$8-

GOLF

A VISUAL HISTORY

***The First Amateur Golf Championship Held
In America, 1894, lithograph after Everett
Henry, 1931***

*This lithograph (by E. Currier) appeared in
Fortune magazine in 1931, and is based on a
drawing by Everett Henry (1893–1961).*

*The records tell us that this cannot have been the
first U.S. Amateur Championship, but the fact that
the players shown are among the earliest champions
of the American game is not in doubt. Charles Blair
Macdonald, famous both as a player and, in later
years, a course designer, is the player striking the
ball, and among those watching are pipe-smoking
John Reid, inspiration behind the celebrated St
Andrew's Golf Club, founded in 1888, and
Laurence Stoddart, victor over Macdonald in one
of the last invitation matches before the founding
of the United States Golf Association.*

GOLF

A VISUAL HISTORY

Michael Hobbs

CRESCENT BOOKS
New York

This 1992 edition published by Crescent
Books, distributed by Outlet Book Company,
Inc., a Random House Company, 225 Park
Avenue South, New York, New York 10003.

Printed in Italy by OFFSET INVICTA Spa
Limena (Padova)

ISBN 0-517-06684-X

8 7 6 5 4 3 2 1

CONTENTS

INTRODUCTION

What is the essence of the game of golf? Some people would immediately think of the final task in playing a golf hole – rather gently tapping a small whitish ball into a hole. However, the real origins of golf almost certainly had nothing whatsoever to do with this, which was a later development.

Early golf was probably essentially a cross-country game, where the prime aim was to move the ball considerable distances with each stroke with the object of reaching the eventual target in as few strokes as possible.

Such a game is reported at Loenen aan de Vecht in northern Holland as early as 1297. In it there were two teams of four players who struck the ball alternately. The course consisted of only four 'holes' but measured a formidable 4,850 yards. The ball would almost certainly have been made of wood, and it would have taken a good free swing and a precise strike to carry it much over 80 yards. With accuracy of direction also needed over rough ground and everyone having to play the ball as it lay, you can work out for yourselves the likely number of strokes which would have been taken to get around the whole course.

The final target was not a hole but the doors of an important building. In much later years the great Ben Hogan would have much preferred this. He, and others like him, have felt that far too much emphasis has been given to putting and to that small hole as golf developed over the centuries.

Winter Landscape, Aert van der Neer,
c.1600
This painting, usually called 'Winter Landscape'
is by Aert van der Neer and shows golf-like games
in progress on a frozen Dutch river.

Les Amusements de l'Hiver, engraving, French, 18th century, after Adriaen van der Velde: Winter Landscape, Golfers on the Ice near Haarlem, 1668
This is an important picture historically. The inclusion of a player in a kilt has been used as evidence that the Scots picked up the idea of the game while trading, or as sailors, in the Low Countries. Again, the game is taking place on the ice but the club about to be used looks capable of hitting the ball a very fair distance. Would he have cried 'Fore!'?

They feel that the true thrill of the game lies in the long game, with the ball flying through the air. Putting is mere scraping along the ground. For those who are so minded, that 4¼ inch hole is nowhere near as good a destination as an iron-banded door of a fortress.

This kind of game persisted in the Low Countries over the centuries but eventually died away; what remained concentrated instead on the finishing element and became more of a court game, effectively a putting contest.

Meanwhile, what had the Scots been doing? Until not so long ago, unknowledgeable journalists used to speculate that the game originated there. They were apt to suppose that the shepherd's crook was the first club and that it was used to swing at roundish stones at times when sheep and lambs were quietly occupied nibbling the turf. But a little reflection makes it seem improbable that shepherds should be given the credit. After all, a common walking stick is considerably more suitable for striking anything whatsoever than a shepherd's crook, which is too long by far.

No one knows when the game was first played in Scotland. Nor whether it developed there quite separately in the Middle Ages or whether the concept was brought back from the Low Countries through the trading links between the two lands. There is, however, no doubt that Scotland is the home of golf in the sense that it was the country from which the game spread. In large part, this was because golfing Scotsmen wanted to continue to play where they went to colonize or work – in the United States, in India, in France and, of course, over the border in England.

The first reference to the game in Scotland itself comes in 1457 when the parliament of King James II 'decreed and ordained that the Fute-ball and Golfe be utterly cryed downe, and not to be used'. There were the hated English to fight in pitched battle, and golf was not much of a preparation. So, instead of golf and football, the king decreed that his people should pay more attention – if they were under 50 and more than 12 – to 'schutting', that is, archery.

We can speculate that the game must have become reasonably popular by that year to be worth the royal ban. His successor returned to the subject in 1471 declaring that these two sports 'be abused [abandoned] in time cumming and schuting used'.

The decrees did not entirely work. In 1491 James IV tried again: 'in na place of the Realme there be used Fute-ball, Golfe, or uther sik unproffitable sports'. But some time later, this king became the first person to be recorded by name as playing the game. Perhaps it serves him right that he was killed in battle against the English.

The game might have been 'unproffitable' in terms of improving Scottish skills with the long bow, but it has long since ceased to be unprofitable in other ways. In the years around the turn of this century, proficiency at the game enabled each of the Great Triumvirate of J.H. Taylor, James Braid and Harry Vardon to become as prosperous as a moderately successful owner of a corner grocery store would have been. Money was not a prime concern to such as Walter Hagen and Bobby Jones in the inter-war years, but all was to change with the arrival of Arnold Palmer on the golfing scene in the late 1950s. In 'profit' terms, he was largely responsible for the revival of the U.S. Tour, the Open Championship and the U.S. Seniors Tour. He might have lacked a graceful swing, been unable to keep his trousers securely fixed to his waist and, in his best playing years, dressed with a total – and commendable – absence of colour co-ordination, but the crowd adored him, and paid to see him play.

Palmer was the first man to make golf pay in millions of dollars. Nearly 30 years after his greatest years, his successors, once they have won a major or two, have fortunes thrust upon them.

For the mass of golfers, profit never was, and never will be, what the game is all about. All the same, money was a necessary part of the game as it developed, as it still is today. In Japan, for example, membership of a club can easily cost $300,000. For centuries the game was far too expensive for the working man to play, even if he had had the spare time, largely because the cost of golf balls was very high. Crude wooden balls might not have cost much to make, but they were succeeded by 'featheries' around 1600. These had a leather cover and were stuffed exceedingly tightly with 'a lum hat full of goose feathers'. A man could make perhaps four a day and they cost as much as a golf club.

In 1848, rubber balls were first made from Malayan gutta percha, and they rapidly became popular. Much cheaper than featheries, they made the game more possible for all. To this day, the golf ball is far more important than any other single element in the development of the game. What does it matter what you hit with, and where you are hitting, compared with the object struck? So, the highly unsatisfactory wooden ball was followed by the excellent

feathery – excellent, that is, as long as you did not mind the cost and did not strike it with the edge of your club, when it would split apart, as it also did in wet weather.

But the gutta percha ball, though excellent for the short game, was difficult to get into the air, and had to be struck from the middle of the club. Towards the end of the last century, from the United States and Coburn Haskell, came the ball with a wound rubber core. Though now long ago, it was the most significant invention of modern times, exceeding even the importance of the steel shafts introduced towards the end of the 1920s, and certainly the technical developments of more recent years.

No implements survive from the earliest years of the game, and there is even less in the way of detailed descriptions of the game or the players. The earliest clubs we have that can be dated with any confidence are in the Royal Troon Golf Club. They were probably made around or before 1741, although others have been found which most likely belong to the previous century. But in terms of what they tell us of the game they were used for, they are mute. So, as regards detail of the early game of golf, are those prohibitions of those far-off Stuart kings of Scotland. 'Don't do it,' the kings said. Their (fortunately ignored) edicts provide no evidence of how the game was played by those distant Scotsmen who ought to have been practising their martial arts.

We live in a visual age. We tend to believe that words can never reveal quite as much as pictures. It may be true that there are few words from the earliest days of golf, but it has always attracted artists. We have images from as long ago as the Middle Ages that show a game that at least resembles golf.

Golf Balls

Changes in golf ball design have had a dramatic effect on the game of golf. It is thought that around 1600 the simple wooden ball went out of use, superseded by the spectacular invention (probably in Holland) of stuffing a hide case tight with feathers – hence the feathery. Then came gutta percha in 1848 and the feathery went out of use almost overnight. Rubber balls were relatively cheap and golf was able to become a mass sport. At the turn of the century, the American Coburn Haskell invented the wound ball. This made the game far more pleasurable for less talented golfers because it demanded less exact striking and less power than the gutta percha ball.

This display at Gullane Golf Club shows the sometimes weird and wonderful variety of golf balls available over the years. We start with a couple of featheries, which are followed by a pair of hand-hammered balls. It was found that the first smooth gutta percha balls did not fly at all well and their performance much improved once they had been nicked during play. It was logical to incorporate such marks right from the start. Ever since, there has been much research into what kinds of markings most improve the aerodynamics of the golf ball.

Then, with the development in the Low Countries in the 17th century of a middle class which had enough time for leisure, there are several more paintings of another game that was similar to golf. While Europe busied itself in the next century with wars, revolutions and colonization, the visual record goes almost as quiet as the written one, until widerspread prosperity again meant that more people not only had time to play, but the money to buy artistic renditions of their favourite pursuit. From the mid-19th century we have the first records of the modern game, and the floodgates for golfing art were simultaneously opened.

Since then, artists have been captivated by the game, the beauty of its setting and the elegance of its play. But not only artists: golf so entered our way of life that it appears on magazine covers, in political cartoons, on fashion plates, in advertisements, indeed anywhere open to graphic images. Although the last hundred years have seen no shortage of words to describe the game, images have provided a gloss to them, and a record every bit as eloquent and as poetic.

The proliferation of the game coincided happily not only with the growth of a market for sporting art, but with the spread of photography. One of the most redolent images we have of the mid-19th century game is not a painting at all but a photograph, taken at Leith in 1867. Over the last hundred years photographers have rarely been far from the great players as they practise their craft. The development of fast shutter speeds, highspeed, fine grain colour film, and telephoto lenses has frozen every pore and sinew of the game, and left a full album of every historic moment.

Pictures may or may not say more than words. But one thing is sure. They provide their own intriguing history of the game that is not the same as the written record. They fill in the gaps where the words do not survive, and add a different interpretation and angle, and their very own breath of reality, where they do.

THE ORIGINS OF THE GAME

Early images of golf are rare – they are for any subject. There exists an early painting of several Chinese ladies playing a game with implements that at least look like golf clubs (it is in fact the traditional game of *suigan*), but the earliest convincing representation of someone playing a game that could be golf is a scene from a stained glass window dating back to about 1350. The window is the East Window (often called the Crecy Window) of Gloucester Cathedral. The player's swing does look like a golf swing, although the club itself is more like a hockey stick, and the ball is too large. So while it would be delightful to believe that this is a depiction of golf, it is unlikely. It is probably a medieval game known as *chole* that involved two teams hitting a ball long distances to an agreed finishing point. Even so, the player, as modern instruction dictates, has made an excellent shoulder movement while restricting his hip turn. That is golf, not hockey – but was very likely *chole* as well.

But for the romantics, perhaps it is a representation of golf after all, with the artist, as was common at that time, much exaggerating the size of the ball and also not recalling accurately the shape of a golf club.

This apart, most of the images of early golf-like games derive from the Low Countries. Fortunately this was at a time when Dutch painting was at a peak, especially when depicting either domestic scenes or active figures in a landscape. Many such scenes are rich in providing glimpses of the game when the painter was interested in something quite different.

So, we have, for example, a house interior with someone holding a golf club, or golf in progress seen through an open door, as in the Rembrandt engraving 'The Kolven Player' of 1654. Better known still are frozen river or lake scenes, with all sorts of everyday things happening in them, among them a form of golf.

This should not lead us to think that the Dutch were primarily ice golfers. Golf was a well-established pastime. It was played around the streets, in a town square, over the fields, and yes, when it was cold, on the ice also. The pictures that derive from this school have a claim to be the most interesting of all golf paintings, both artistically and historically. The Dutch decorative tiles of the period hold a similar fascination.

No such early paintings exist from Scotland. To date, the earliest known is Paul Sandby's most enjoyable work from 1746 which shows men in tricorne hats playing on Bruntsfield links with Edinburgh Castle in the backgound. There is also a milkmaid in the painting and one can speculate that Sandby had not the slightest interest in golf. He was painting a distant view of the castle with a bucolic foreground. He wanted some figures, and the golfers made his grand design more lively.

As we will see, things were soon to change. Golf grabbed the attention and became the primary focus of many a painting, both portrait and landscape – a development we must put down to the remarkable strides the game made in 18th century Scotland, and particularly along the East coast.

(Below) **Ice on the Scheldt, Artist Unknown, 17th century**
This painting, sometimes attributed to Adriaen van der Velde, is usually called 'Ice on the Scheldt'. It was presented to the Royal and Ancient by Lord Boothby shortly after World War II.

(Right) **Pleasures of Ice, Esaias van de Velde, c.1600**
Prints of this popular painting first appeared in Bernard Darwin's A Golfer's Gallery of Old Masters *(a book of reproductions much sought after by collectors). This time, the golf-like game is attracting the attention of most of the figures in the painting.*

(Right) **Game on the Ice, Antonie van Straelen, 17th century**
Here Antonie van Straelen shows people taking their pleasure on what appears to be the frozen expanses of a flooded river. Golf, or a golf-like game, is the centre of attention. Four figures watch the outcome of what looks to have been a putt (judging by the lack of follow-through from the player).

(Left and detail below) **The Crecy Window, Gloucester Cathedral, c.1350**
The East Window of Gloucester Cathedral, often known as the Crecy Window because of its association with the battle of that name, contains a small roundel which has caught the attention of golf historians. The figure is playing a game with a stick and a ball, and his swing does suggest a golf swing. We can only speculate as to the game he was playing — a kind of cross-country golf?

(Right) **Chinese Ladies Playing a Golf-Type Game, Ming Era (1368 – 1644)**
Despite any romantic hopes, this game is hardly golf-like, let alone golf. These Chinese ladies are playing a game called suigan. *Clearly it was an indoor or garden game and hardly more similar to the cross-country game of golf than billiards. However, they are using implements quite like golf clubs and the picure is interesting for showing how widespread through both history and geography is the idea of playing a game involving sticks and balls.*

The Kolven Player, Rembrandt van Rijn, 1654

Can golf claim to have attracted the attention of one of the world's greatest artists – Rembrandt van Rijn? Although Rembrandt is mainly interested in the figure at rest, this glimpse through the doorway of a street or courtyard game is drawn sufficiently casually to suggest that there was nothing unusual about the game being played. It is safe to assume it is a golf-like game much like those depicted on frozen lakes and rivers.

An Ice Scene, Antonie van Straelen, Dutch, 17th century
Dutch landscape painters quite often featured a form of golf as details in their work. Here the painter seems far more interested in the trees and buildings than the two boys putting.

Les Nouvelles Règles pour le Jeu de Mail, French, 1717

New rules for the game of Mail were published in 1717. Though the game does not appear to be a very close relation of golf, being more like croquet, there are resemblances, and as a result, high prices at auction are paid by golf collectors for anything connected with the history of this game. It is interesting to note that sports were being taken sufficiently seriously for rules to be written down and published.

The Macdonald Boys, Jeremiah Davison, 1741

The Lord Macdonald of the Isles with his brother, Sir James Macdonald of Sleat, was painted by Jeremiah Davison (or Davidson). To create a feeling of relaxation, the painter introduced some props, among them a sporting gun and a wooden golf club, probably a playclub (driver). Sir James's grip is very likely the one generally in use, the hands slightly separated with the right otherwise quite modern in positioning, while the left looks in what is normally called a 'weak' position, the back of the hand facing down the target line.

Golf on Bruntsfield Links, Paul Sandby, 1746

Paul Sandby (1725 – 1809) may have painted the first British golf picture (unfortunately no longer in the best condition). It is unlikely that he had the slightest interest in golf; he was probably more interested in the distant prospect of Edinburgh. In the foreground, he needed some figures to give perspective and liveliness. So he put in a cowherd and some golfers. Have the golfers possibly upset the cows?

THE GAME ESTABLISHED

As has already been said, we do not know, nor are we ever likely to know, exactly where and when golf was first played in Scotland. Nevertheless, we can assert with some confidence that early development was almost certainly confined to the eastern seaboard and nearby. St Andrews in Fife is often referred to as 'the home of golf'. It certainly is in terms of the town's and the Royal and Ancient Golf Club's influence on the development of the game, and there is evidence of the game being played on what is now known as the Old Course in the mid-16th century. However, as we have seen, the kings of Scotland were banning the game earlier than that, which indicates that golf must have had a popularity at least widespread enough to be noticeable.

Mention of the game mostly derives from household accounts, minor court cases and, more rarely, books. Take Dornoch as an example. In 1616 the Earl of Sutherland's accounts note expenditure on 'bows, arrows, golfclubs and balls', while Sir Robert Gordon wrote at about the same time: 'About this town along the sea coast are the fairest and largest links or green fields of any part of Scotland. Fit for archery, golfing, riding and exercises they do surpass the fields of Montrose or St Andrews.' This remark also confirms that these two towns were already golfing centres. There is broadly similar evidence for Banff, Aberdeen, Carnoustie, and Leven (in Fife), although

undoubtedly the main centre for golf in the 17th century was the Edinburgh area, with golf being played in distant view from the castle at Bruntsfield and also Leith and Musselburgh. Golf was also played further inland at Perth, a surprising venue before grass-cutting machinery became available. The explanation is that they played only out of the grass-growing season.

Clubs were not formed until the 18th century. Two claim to be the earliest: the Royal Burgess Golfing Society of Edinburgh, which regards the year 1735 as the date of its foundation, and the Honourable Company of Edinburgh Golfers, whose minutes begin in 1744, and who are also the first known source for rules of golf. The Royal and Ancient dates from slightly later – 1754.

Club captains became key figures in the organization of the game at an early stage, and we owe to the tradition of painting club captains some of the most potent of early golfing images. It is of course a tradition that continues through to the present day, and in the case of such clubs as the Royal Liverpool at Hoylake photographs of their captains go back to the 19th century. The custom, however, dates back earlier still to the years either side of 1800, and to some of the most popular of all golf paintings. Lemuel Francis Abbott's portrait of William Innes, captain of Royal Blackheath, a painting popularly known as 'The

Blackheath Golfer', dates from about 1790. In the years that followed David Allan painted William Inglis, Sir George Chalmers painted William St Clair of Roslin, and Sir John Watson Gordon painted John Taylor. All are powerful images, with each man standing in ceremonial attire.

By the end of the 18th century, there were still only seven clubs in the whole of the United Kingdom, and growth was slow until the enormous expansion of interest in sport in later Victorian times. Then the statistics are remarkable. In 1870 there were 34 clubs. That number had nearly doubled by 1880, and in 1890 had reached 387. In 1900 there were well over 2,000, and over 4,000 by the time of World War I.

From being a sport played by the few in a very few areas of Scotland, golf had by then become something that was essential to the life of every small town through the United Kingdom, with courses by the dozen clustering around major cities. It had already begun to spread well beyond the confines of the British Isles, taking particular root in the English-speaking world.

The trigger for the establishment of golf as a popular game was the invention of the relatively cheap gutta percha ball in 1848. That initial growth accelerated, as in so many other sporting fields, with an increase in leisure for the middle class, while the more traditionally leisured widened their interests beyond mainly field sports.

As golf became more visible it was painted more and then photographed. For most the work was very occasional, perhaps a golfing scene which took their fancy on a summer's day while on holiday. Keen golfers such as Thomas Hodges and Francis Powell Hopkins ('Shortspoon'), who were also amateur artists, were far more prolific. They must have found a ready market among their fellow golfers, even if it was not very rewarding in monetary terms. Hopkins was, most likely, the first man to depict golfers in action, but his work is at its most interesting when it shows such scenes as assemblages of golfers at Blackheath in 1875 or Westward Ho! in 1877.

The increasing number of golfing portraits, as opposed to landscapes, were probably more lucrative, and as time passed the field widened beyond those proud and self-satisfied looking captains mentioned earlier. The rather crude depiction of Willie Park Senior setting up to the ball is particularly interesting because it is so early, perhaps painted shortly after he won the first Open Championship in 1860. Far more frequently painted was Tom Morris, once he had become the Grand Old Man of golf, and he also appears in many photographs and photogravures.

Since that period, all the great players have been photographed frequently, with paintings becoming a rarity. One can only guess how many frames of transparency film are exposed of a player with the appeal of Seve Ballesteros – surely some millions every year. Paintings of the great players of the first half of the century nonetheless do exist, and there has happily been a quite recent surge of interest in portraying the moderns.

(Left) **The Society of Golfers at Blackheath, Lemuel Francis Abbott, 1790**
Popularly called 'The Blackheath Golfer', this is the most famous golf painting of them all and never loses its appeal. It shows William Innes (1719 – 95) in the garb of club captain of Royal Blackheath (south-east of London), the first club to be founded in England. Recent research has demonstrated that the original painting was destroyed in the Indian Mutiny and this mezzotint was first produced by Valentine Green in 1790.

It was the first golf painting reproduced as a print. The original print was not coloured, but it has appeared in various versions over the years. Note also the clubs: a valuable insight into what was in use at the time.

(Right) **William Inglis, David Allan, 1787**
David Allan (1744 – 96) painted a captain of the Honourable Company of Edinburgh Golfers, William Inglis, in 1787. The background is Leith Links. Inglis is grasping his playclub (driver) in his right hand and it is interesting evidence of what such a club looked like. In the background, we can see that the links are not solely devoted to golf but, just to the right of Inglis's left thigh we can see that the big competition for the silver club was imminent as it is being paraded with two drummers.

The first competition for the silver club was played over Leith Links on 2 April 1744 and was won by the Edinburgh surgeon John Rattray. He has therefore a claim to be recognized as the first champion golfer of them all.

The city of Edinburgh presented the club but were insistent that there should be no further expense 'except to intimate by Tuck of Drum, through the City, the day upon which it shall be annually played'. In later years, the city did incur further expense, presenting two more silver clubs, but they did not have to pay for the silver balls which were attached after each victory.

William St Clair of Roslin, Sir George Chalmers, 1791

Sir George Chalmers, who died in 1791, here depicts William St Clair of Roslin, who was captain of the Honourable Company of Edinburgh Golfers in 1761, 1766, 1770, and 1771 and also a Grand Master Mason of Scotland. The original now hangs at the Royal Company of Archers building in Edinburgh, highly appropriate because he may well have been even more expert in archery than golf. The Honourable Company sold the painting in the 19th century at a time when they were hard-up to the point of extinction. They retain a fine copy.

We cannot be sure that William St Clair actually stood to the ball like this. If he did, he would surely have played with a low flight – useful in high winds – and been plagued by a duck hook. He died in 1778.

John Taylor, Sir John Watson Gordon, early 19th century

John Taylor is here captured by Sir John Watson Gordon (1788 – 1864), the leading Scottish portrait painter of the time. It has been argued that at least some of the painting may have been carried out by an even greater name, Sir Henry Raeburn.

Taylor was one of the most formidable golfers of the Edinburgh area and was eight times captain of the Honourable Company of Edinburgh Golfers during the first quarter of the 19th century.

Henry Callender, Lemuel Francis Abbott, 1807
Here Abbott depicts another Blackheath golfer, Henry Callender, who was captain of Royal Blackheath in 1807.

'Old Alick', Robert Samuel Ennis Gallon, 1830s

This painting by Robert Samuel Ennis Gallon (or Gallen) is owned by Royal Blackheath. It depicts 'Old Alick' (Alick Brotherstone) who was appointed hole cutter on the club's course in 1822. This might not seem an onerous job but no simple device to take the skill out of the job had been invented by this time. Brotherstone had to use a knife, and his neatness was much respected, as was his past as a sailor on various of Admiral Horatio Nelson's ships.

The Ruling Passion, C. Thomas, 1823
This is a sly comment on the difference between old age and youth. The old gentlemen's passion is golf, while in the background the young couple's passion is something quite different.

Young Boy in Landscape, early 19th century
This painting, which comes from the feather ball era, has a particular appeal for the collectors of early golf clubs. As with The Macdonald Boys, *it is basically a portrait with the mountain backcloth and the introduction of the club making the scene more natural. The date is speculative but the picturesque setting suggests early 19th century.*

A Winter Evening, W. Dendy Sadler
Engraved by James Dobie after a painting by Sadler, this is sometimes called 'A Winter Evening' and also 'A Caddie to the Royal and Ancient'. The man is depicted cleaning his master's clubs. The painting was carried out around the time of the beginning of World War I but harks back to an earlier period – from the shape of the woods, about 1850, before Sadler (1854 – 1923) was born. A sentimental painting, it reflects his interest in costume pictures.

Golf at Bruntsfield, Jock Barclay, c.1830
Bruntsfield Links (which was not a links at all) is one of the key places where the early golfers of Edinburgh used to gather. This atmospheric painting is by Old Jock Barclay, and shows the castle in the background.

(Left) **Sketch for The Golfers, Charles Lees, 1841**

Lees was extremely thorough in preparing this painting, and did detailed sketches of every individual. Some of these were reproduced in 1907 in H.S.C. Everard's A History of the Royal and Ancient Golf Club. *This sketch is of William Goddard of Leith, a very good amateur of his time.*

(Right) **The Golfers: A Grand Match Played Over St Andrews Links, Charles Lees, 1841**
This has claim to be the most sought-after, and most valuable, of all golf paintings. It remains, however, in the possession of a descendant of one of the spectators portrayed.

Painted by Charles Lees (1800 – 80), it depicts a foursome match involving four well-known St Andrews golfers on the Old Course. It not only shows the players, but in the tradition of Victorian paintings of crowds, depicts some 50 spectators in considerable detail. The Golfers also has a particular significance, because of the evidence it provides that for some artists at least golf and golfers were now fit subjects to be centre-stage — and not subordinate to the landscape, or indeed the sheep.

Willie Park Senior (detail), anon, c.1860
This representation of Willie Park Senior was for a long time in the Park family and almost certainly depicts him shortly after he had won an early British Open, perhaps the first of all. He later added the 1863, 1866 and 1875 championships. At that time matchplay was considered to be far more important than tournaments, and the matches he played over the years attracted much more public interest.

Mr Francis Bennoch, Captain of the Royal Blackheath Golf Club, 1860 – 61

This portrait of Francis Bennoch, is taken from Bernard Darwin's A Golfer's Gallery. *Golf historians find considerable evidence about golf equipment, especially the clubs used in the past, from books such as Darwin's. It is also interesting to compare this portrait with those of earlier Royal Blackheath captains and note the striking similarities.*

Grand Golf Tournament, Leith, 1867

This is one of two famous photographs taken at a Grand Golf Tournament played over Leith Links in 1867. Perhaps its main interest is that this photograph contains one of the few images of that brief comet, Young Tom Morris, to have survived. Then about 16 years old, he leans on the railings at the back right of the steps. Most photographs of his father show Old Tom in the 1890s or early this century, but this is how the man looked when he was winning his four Open Championships. He is at the bottom of the steps, below his son. To his right is the 1865 Open Champion, Andrew Strath.

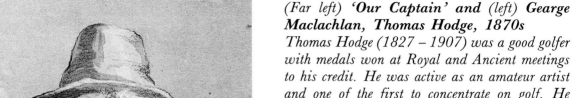

"George" Maclachlan.

(Far left) **'Our Captain' and** *(left)* **Gearge Maclachlan, Thomas Hodge, 1870s**
Thomas Hodge (1827 – 1907) was a good golfer with medals won at Royal and Ancient meetings to his credit. He was active as an amateur artist and one of the first to concentrate on golf. He contributed to the Badminton Golf *and other publications.*

Young Tom's Last Match, Francis Powell Hopkins, 1875
One of the fabled moments in golfing history, this unlikely match in the snow between Young Tom Morris and Arthur Molesworth was the last Young Tom was to play. In his short life he won the Open four times, and it must have been with some pride that his father, caddying for him on this occasion, watched him play.

The tragic death of Young Tom at the age of 24, less than a month after this match, is usually linked to the death that autumn of his wife in giving birth to a still-born child, though his death certificate indicated the cause of death as a lung haemorrhage.

Golfers, Clark Stanton, 1875
Two Royal and Ancient amateurs portrayed in oil by Clark Stanton. The club carrier is Allan Robertson, generally reckoned to be the outstanding player of his day and the first great professional. Note the red jackets, often worn by golfers of this time.

Putting, William Edwin Pimm c.1900

Some uncertainty surrounds the identity of this painting. There is no doubt that the painting is by Pimm, a painter active around the turn of the last century, but the subject has caused some puzzlement.

In all probability the man putting is Dr Laidlaw Purves, a Scot resident in London who played regularly at the Royal Wimbledon Club. The wearing of the red jacket could be explained by the fact that until 1907 the Royal Wimbledon Club played on Wimbledon Common itself: the wearing of red jackets was obligatory. Pimm's partner is thought to be Arthur Molesworth.

(Above) **Tom Morris, James Patrick, c. 1890 and** *(left)* **Tom Morris, John I. McClymont, 1900**

Old Tom Morris was the most photographed and painted player of his time. This was partly because he lived a long life and came to occupy much the same position in golf as did W.G. Grace at a similar time in cricket, and Babe Ruth later in baseball.

He played in every Open Championship from 1860 to 1896, winning it four times, and coming second in the first ever Open (Willie Park was the winner). From 1864 he was professional at St Andrews, where he became a part of the scenery, which is one reason why he was painted and photographed so often. The watercolour by James Patrick depicts him about to play from a bunker with the Royal and Ancient clubhouse behind him. The McClymont oil poses him thoughtfully in front of the course.

Tom Morris Outside His Shop

A hand-coloured postcard showing Tom Morris outside his shop at St Andrews. The shop still exists hard by the 18th green on the Old Course, although it has been considerably modernized. It was here that Robert Lockhart bought the clubs and balls used in the first modern game of golf in the U.S.

The Thoughtful   The Nervous   The Deadly

Puts and Putters

Puts and Putters, Francis Powell Hopkins (Major Shortspoon)

This watercolour is by Francis Powell Hopkins. Note the signature: he signed himself Major Shortspoon or Major S on watercolours which he must have thought slighter works. Oils were more significant works and therefore signed F.P. Hopkins. A short spoon was roughly equivalent to today's 3-wood but had a shorter shaft than a standard spoon. He presumably chose the name because this was his favourite club. In these three portraits of putting, golfing friends or acquaintances were probably his models.

Hopkins played golf a great deal at Westward Ho! and gave five times Open Champion J.H. Taylor his first job – caddying. Taylor wrote many years later: 'I caught a real Tartar. Major Hopkins was a delightful Irishman whose genial qualities were overshadowed by extreme irascibility.'

That first outing as a caddie should have earned Taylor 6 old pence (10 cents). However, the major reduced the fee by half because Taylor, impeded by short-sightedness, failed to find an errant ball.

Years later, Taylor bought a collection of the major's paintings and gave them to the club, Royal North Devon. He paid a relatively small sum, in contrast to the high prices they would fetch today.

Swilcan Bridge, St Andrews, Francis Powell Hopkins
There is a comical element in many if not most of Francis Powell Hopkins' paintings. This is one of his versions of a golfer who has got himself into the Swilcan Burn, a stream that is still a famous hazard on the Old Course at St Andrews.

Portrait of an Unknown Golfer, Francis Powell Hopkins
This oil is probably of one of Shortspoon's golfing acquaintances or friends, but he remains anonymous.

(Below) **Prestwick,** (below left) **Musselburgh and** (left) **North Berwick, Francis Powell Hopkins**

Prestwick was the club that initiated the Open Championship. However, it has never applied to stage the event again since crowd problems at the climax of the 1925 Open. As is the case with the final few holes at Hoylake, there is not the acreage to accommodate the huge crowds that can, at times, be swallowed up among the dunes of a course such as Birkdale. Judging by the sleepered bunker to the right, this golfer is just about to attempt to make the carry at the Himalayas Hole. Musselburgh and North Berwick are two more among the many Scottish courses painted by Hopkins.

(Below) **Hell Bunker, Old Course St Andrews, John Smart, 1880s**

John Smart produced paintings of Scottish golf scenes during the late 1880s which George Aikman engraved, for a limited edition book, The Golf Greens of Scotland. *At this time, it is likely that Hell Bunker on the 14th on the Old Course was merely ill-kept, but Smart has made it seem both more formidable and convolutedly picturesque. The resultant picture is pleasantly balanced between this formidable hazard and the distant St Andrews skyline. The golfers feature with less significance.*

(Right) **The Tee Shot (The First Tee at Westward Ho!), Francis Powell Hopkins**

This famous painting was commissioned by John Dun, a Liverpool banker and the Captain of the Royal Liverpool Golf Club. It was later presented to the Royal North Devon Golf Club by his son. Dun is driving off and Captain Molesworth is waiting his turn.

'. . . recently the amusing sketches of Major Shortspoon have been in great demand hence the desire for a modern golf picture; but to produce one without an incident and to make it interesting is an achievement of high art. This the Major has succeeded in doing admirably' – The Field.

Hill Hole, Luffness, John Smart, 1889
Luffness is hard by the three courses at Gullane, to the east of Edinburgh. This John Smart painting shows a golfer about to play his tee shot at the Hill Hole in 1889.

Gullane, John Smart, 1880
This is the original watercolour from which the engraving was made for Smart and Aikman's The Golf Greens of Scotland.

Gullane, Robert Buchanan Nisbet, 1880

Gullane is an East Lothian village, with three golf courses (and others close by), which seems to revolve around golf. This watercolour from 1880 is by Robert Buchanan Nisbet RSA (1857 – 1942). The scene is not vastly changed today except that visitors from far and wide flock to play Gullane 1, 2 and 3, while Luffness New is a stone's throw away and Muirfield just down the road.

Gullane has a long history of golf. As long ago as 1650 there was an annual match on Gullane Hill between the weavers of Dirleton and of Aberlady, and a regular golf club was founded in the 1800s. It benefited much from the coming of the railway, and this popularity perhaps accounts for why it has been much painted.

The First Meeting of the Gullane Golf Club, 1882
The first meeting of the current Gullane Golf Club in 1882. Caddies were usually asked to join in for the group picture on such occasions, showing how they had become an integral adjunct to the gentleman's pursuit.

St Andrews, 1885
Photographs can be much more intriguing than paintings. What does this scene outside the Royal and Ancient clubhouse at St Andrews depict? It is obviously staged and the photographer has told everyone to look very interested. The boy and the woman to the left could not have cared less!

MAY 6TH 1885   No 1

St Andrews, Robert Buchanan Nisbet, 1880
This watercolour shows St Andrews painted from across the Firth of Forth. The skyline of 'the old grey town' is little changed today, but the Old Course is now far better ordered. The players seem successfully to have passed Hell Bunker (in the foreground) and are about to play to the 14th green.

Swilcan Bridge, St Andrews, John Barclay, late 19th century
The golfers have played their tee shots up the final fairway on the Old Course, St Andrews. Here the pair go, followed by their caddies. This charming lithograph is the only impression.

The Cheerful Caddy Boy, J.M. Singleton, late 19th century
Distinctly of the chocolate box school, this painting of a caddie by J.M. Singleton comes from the 1880s or, more likely, the 1890s, when carrying bags came in. Sadly, the clubs are not painted quite well enough for much information to be derived from them.

Golf at Prestwick, c.1890
Note the two caddies. The one nearer the centre of
the picture is carrying clubs in the traditional way
– under the arm. Golf bags were, however, coming
to be the fashion and the other caddy is much more
up-to-date.

John Ball Lining Up a Putt on the 9th Hole at Hoylake, Ionicus

'Ionicus' (otherwise Jos Armitage, perhaps best known for his P.G. Wodehouse illustrations) is a long-time member of Royal Liverpool Golf Club at Hoylake. He has been drawn to the career of one of the club's most famous members, John Ball, winner of eight Amateur Championships and also the first English winner of the Open in 1890. Here Ball is considering his putt on the 9th at his home club.

Hoylake is the fourth oldest course in England, having been set out in 1869 by George Morris. However, its claim to historical importance is even greater than that, as two of its predecessors, Royal Blackheath and Old Manchester, no longer play on their original sites.

John Ball lining up a putt on the 9th hole (Punch Bowl) at Hoylake

(Left) The Ginger Beer Hole, William Blake Lamond, 1894

The names of many holes on golf courses suggest that they derive from a committee. They seldom catch on with club members. Those that do seem to arrive spontaneously and are usually prosaic: The Gasworks, The Pit, The Ponds, and The Quarry are examples. Lamond shows a group of golfers taking their ease after playing the 4th on the Old Course at St Andrews. The liquid is ginger beer, and the 4th acquired that name because of the nearby stall that used to dispense the drink.

(Right) The Drive, Charles Edmund Brock, 1894

Charles Edmund Brock (1870 – 1938) produced three golf paintings in 1894 which were then issued as engravings. The three were 'The Drive', 'The Putt' and 'The Bunker'. If the caddies are perhaps sentimentalized, the driver is presented in a very lively fashion.

(Left) **Golfers in Elizabethan Dress, anon, c.1900**

James II is recorded as having played golf, and so, too, was Charles I earlier in the 17th century. As people in late Victorian times became more curious about the past of the sport, several artists showed golfers in historical costume. There is also an element of humour in the notion that the famous figures of history were much like us.

The Sabbath Breakers, John Charles Dollman, 1896

We can learn snippets of golf history from court and parish records. Playing golf was not allowed by the Church in Scotland for much of the game's history, and playing while morning church services were in progress was an even worse sin.

This painting by John Charles Dollman (1851 – 1934) shows an incident when a certain

John Henrie and Pat Rogie were discovered transgressing on Leith Links in 1592. Such historical paintings became popular as golf spread and a market for golf-related objects and paintings grew.

Sandy, 'C.E.D.'
This watercolour of a well-known caddie at the turn of the last century is full of character. Some caddies became famous names in their own right 'Big' Crawford was one and 'Fiery' John Carey another.

'Fiery' John Carey, c.1900
'Fiery' John Carey was known as 'Fiery' because of his reddish complexion, though, given his dour countenance there may have been a touch of humour in the nickname. He caddied for some of the greatest players of his day, especially Willie Park.

GOLF FINDS NEW HOMES

First the Scots, and later the English, began to spread the game throughout the world, especially the British Empire. Royal Calcutta in India dates from 1829, for example, while Scottish officers played at Pau in southern France after Wellingtons's victorious Peninsular campaign. The first continental European club was established in 1856, in the same town.

Growth was quite rapid in Australia, New Zealand and Canada, but in many countries with Empire connections it was not to be taken up in large numbers by home-grown golfers for many more years. The game was played almost solely by those in temporary exile from the British Isles on account of their work.

The United States was a very different story. Equipment for playing the game is recorded as having been shipped from Leith to South Carolina as early as 1743, and two clubs are known to have been formed in the South before the turn of the century, while an advertisement dating from 1779 offers 'excellent Clubs and Caledonian balls for sale' in New York. Nothing so far has been discovered about the progress of the game there, other than that it evidently died out.

However, it is a joke of history that golf should have perished so quickly after its first arrival in the United States. The second coming was very different. John Reid is usually credited as being the father of American golf because what he began

continued. Any other similar endeavour by anyone else did not survive long.

On Wednesday 14 November, 1888, Scotsman Reid and four friends played golf on six roughly laid out holes set in 30 acres of pastureland. Afterwards, they gathered for dinner in Reid's house and formed the St Andrews Golf Club, based in Yonkers, New York. They then elected Robert Lockhart a member of their new club, which is just as well as he also has claim to being the father of modern American golf. A boyhood friend of Reid in Dunfermline, Scotland, he brought over the clubs with which they had played their game.

This was not quite the first golf they had played. Reid had laid out three very short holes across the road from his house in February of the same year. A few years later, in 1892, he and others established a third course, again six holes. Laid out among apple orchards, it got the group their nickname 'The Apple Tree Gang'. By this time, they had already had their first competition for the club championship, and their first 'nineteenth hole' – an apple tree from which hung a basket of sandwiches and a demijohn of whisky.

The expansion of American golf was swift, with courses at Newport, Rhode Island, and Wheaton, Chicago, and Shinnecock Hills. The first Amateur Championship was played in 1894, as was the first U.S. Open. The women were only a little way behind,

playing in 1895. These early events are not now recognized because they pre-date the founding of the United States Golf Association, but the winners considered themselves champions.

Competitively, most of the early big events were won by Americans who had learned the game in Scotland or by emigré Scots. This soon changed. The United States had her first native American Open Champion, Johnny McDermott, in 1911.

Imported games did not generally take root quickly in the United States. Lawn tennis, at first, was too 'foreign'. Possibly cricket was more successful, but only for a while. Although golf too was foreign, it bucked the trend and rapidly took off, despite being regarded as a game for the well-off. That changed in 1913, only 25 years after the start of golf in America, when a young, working-class amateur, Francis Ouimet, first tied British Open Champions Ted Ray and Harry Vardon (who had won the U.S. Open on his only previous appearance) and then soundly beat them in the 18-hole play-off. He was only 20 years old.

It was an enormous boost to golf. In the higher reaches of the game it made American champions realize that they could beat the British. Once Hagen, Sarazen and Jones had successively achieved their peak games, that is exactly what the Americans did – time and time again – and the

United States was to enjoy a period of international dominance which lasted to the 1980s.

The women's game developed far more easily in America than in Britain, and far more rapidly. As we have seen, the first women's championship in America was played in 1895, when the game was just a few years old. In Britain, with a golf history going back to at least the early 15th century, the first similar championship was played only a couple of years earlier than the American. Women's golf was for a time restricted to little more than long putting, it being thought – by men – unladylike to swing a golf club vigorously, particularly above shoulder height. The first British champion, Lady Margaret Scott, was used to playing with her brothers, all superior golfers. Even she, however, knew the woman's role. When she married, she gave up serious competitive golf.

The First Golf Club in America, 1882
Golf first took root to flourish in North America in Montreal (although we should remember that a much earlier visitation had faded away). Six holes came into play on 7 November 1873, and Queen Victoria granted the Royal title in 1884. The club now has two fine 18 hole courses, both designed by Dick Wilson.

The founder of the club was Alexander Dennitoyn and he appears in this picture of some of the members.

(Left) **'The Old Apple Tree Gang', Leland R. Gustavson, 1896 – 1966**

Gustavson was primarily a magazine illustrator for the Saturday Evening Post *and* McCalls. *He painted several scenes isolating moments in U.S. golf history. The emigré Scot, John Reid, is credited with the creation of golf in the United States (though it was in fact a revival of a forgotten earlier beginning). He laid out a rough three-hole course in Yonkers, New York State in 1888, which then grew quickly from small beginnings. It is now the St Andrews Golf Club and is owned by Jack Nicklaus.*

The apple tree was the clubhouse and suitable drink was kept hanging from a bough.

(Right) **The First Clubhouse in America, Shinnecock Hills, Leland R. Gustavson, 1892**

The first purpose-built golf clubhouses were very small, often made of iron. Otherwise a club would be more likely to have the use of a room in some conveniently placed hotel or inn. Shinnecock Hills, however, had far grander ideas right from the start and engaged a fashionable architect, Stanford White, with this clubhouse as a result. The club itself became a founder member of the United States Golf Association and the course has hosted the U.S. Open in recent years.

(Below) **Awarding the first U.S.G.A. Trophy, Leland R. Gustavson, 1895**
Here Charles Blair Macdonald is shown accepting the U.S. Amateur Championship trophy in 1895 – the first official one because the United States Golf Association had just been formed. Macdonald later won much esteem as a golf architect, a term he himself coined. The painting is by Leland Gustavson, primarily a magazine illustrator, who produced a series of pictures depicting historic moments in U.S. golf history.

(Right) **East Lothian, W.D. McKay, c.1890**
The peacefulness of a near-deserted golf course has often had great appeal to painters. This course is in the Edinburgh area.

Crossing Jordan (Pau), Garden Grant Smith, 1892

Garden Grant Smith was a keen golfer, the editor of the magazine Golf Illustrated, and a painter. During the 19th century Pau, in the south-west of France, became very popular with the English during the winter. Golf had, in fact, first been played there as Wellington's victorious troops moved north after the Peninsular campaign, and the first European golf club was established there in 1856. This quiet scene was painted at a time when golf had become a regular feature of life in Pau.

Pau, Allen C. Sealy, 1893

We do not now know who the players in this picture are. Phil Pilley, in his book Golfing Art, *tells us that there was a key, but that it was lost during the German occupation of the town during World War II. The man putting might be Horace Hutchinson, who had twice won the Amateur Championship the previous decade and was invited everywhere.*

(Left) Gladstone at North Berwick, George Pipeshank, 1895

Golf became the first modern sport in which leading politicians felt happy to participate in public. You would not find a prime minister playing soccer, but the great Victorian prime minister, William Gladstone, has been caught in a bunker by 'George Pipeshank'. The artist's real name was John Wallace (1841–1903), which is how he was known as a painter and lithographer; he used the pseudonym for works he was commissioned to do by the Copes Tobacco Company.

(Below) Political Cartoon, George Pipeshank, 1898

The significance of this painting is now obscure. The Chinese caddie is watched not only by a gallery of familiar Pipeshank figures, but also by an American and a Russian, while a flotilla of battleships can be seen in the background. Deepening the mystery, on the back of the painting there is a poem by the American poet Bret Harte, entitled 'The Partitioning by Truthful James':

Which we had a game
  And Li Hung took a hand,
It was gowffing the same
  He did not understand.
But he smiled as he put down the ball,
  With the smile that was childlike and bland.
Then they looked down at Li,
  And they gazed on the tee,
And each heaved a sigh
  And said, 'Can this be?'
We are ruined by Chinese cheap labour.
  And they want for that Heathen Chinee.

Open Golf Championship, Muirfield, 1896
The Open Championship first came to the home of the Honourable Company of Edinburgh Golfers at Muirfield in 1892, but the course was much criticized and was changed for 1896, when this photograph was taken. It was a momentous event for it saw the sudden emergence of Harry Vardon when J. H. Taylor, having won successive Opens, still had the aura of invincibility. Taylor personally must have felt less than invincible, having recently been defeated by Vardon in a challenge match.

Open Golf Championship, Muirfield, 1896
Harry Vardon, needing a four to beat J.H. Taylor in the Open, decided to play short of a threatening cross bunker near the green and settle for a safe five and a play-off. He then went on to win the 36 hole play-off by four strokes. This photograph shows Taylor about to tee off on the 1st, then a par three.

Harry Vardon is facing him. Almost certainly this photograph was taken at the beginning of the play-off. Although there are quite a number of spectators, it is nevertheless clear that the Open of the 1890s was by no means an event that the world turned out for.

(Left) **Robert Maxwell Waiting to Present the Open Trophy to Harry Vardon, 1896**
Today, hundreds of photographers swarm for the 'the trophy shot' at the U.S. and British Open Championships. When this was taken, there was perhaps only one present, summoned to the scene by the Muirfield club.

(Right) **Amateur Golf Championship, Muirfield, 1897**
A scene from just before the presentation of the trophy for the Amateur Championship at the course of the Honourable Company of Edinburgh Golfers, Muirfield, in 1897. The winner was an Edinburgh University student, A. J. T. Allan, who died the following year. He cycled to the course for each of his matches, removed the clips from his trousers and was off.

Drawing from The Girl's Own Paper, Garden Grant Smith, 1894

Nowadays, women are encouraged to restrict both backswing and hip turns as a means of attempting to generate more clubhead speed. In the early days of women's golf, the fashions in clothing also inflicted a restriction. Quite early this century, women began to wear clothes that were more suitable for the game, but the full change did not come until after World War I.

By the 1890s, golf was being played more by women, and inclusion in a girls' magazine like The Girl's Own Paper *gave it the seal of approval as a suitable pastime for young ladies.*

Silver Cigarette Case, 1898
Artists are often more interested in effect than golfing technique. This cigarette case shows a vigorous player, but his over-long backswing and flying right elbow make the outcome of his shot dubious.

(Left) Saturday Morning, Reiss, John Wallace, 1895
John Wallace is perhaps best known for his cigarette card series. Here he shows a peaceful scene – a Saturday morning's golf at Reiss Golf Club, near Wick, about as far north as you can go in Scotland.

(Right) Then the Schoolboy with his Satchel, John Hassall, 1899
John Hassall (1868 – 1948) produced seven collotypes with the theme 'The Seven Ages of Golf' – parodying Shakespeare's thoughts on man's progress through life from As You Like It. *The original set is a collector's item and now fetches high prices at auction.*

Then The Schoolboy With His Satchel   And Shining Morning Face.

(Left) J.H. Taylor, James Braid, Harry Vardon and Sandy Herd

With the death of Young Tom Morris in 1875 at the age of 24, his equal was not seen again for many a year. That changed when J.H. Taylor became a major force in the mid-1890s. His brief dominance was then challenged very quickly by Harry Vardon, who soon outshone Taylor. Early the following century, James Braid was, for a decade, more successful than either of them, and the term 'The Great Triumvirate' was coined. Here (left to right) we see J.H. Taylor, James Braid and Harry Vardon, together with Sandy Herd, victor in the 1902 British Open.

(Right) The Great Triumvirate, Clement Flower, 1913

This is among the most famous of golf pictures, and was painted by Clement Flower in 1913, just before the war virtually put an end to the careers of (left to right) J.H. Taylor, James Braid and Harry Vardon. At the time, these three members of 'The Great Triumvirate' were of virtually equal stature. Perhaps Flower had historical insight in making Vardon so much the centre of attention of this picture. When it was painted, each had won five Open Championships but Vardon won again in 1914 to put him on the peak that even Peter Thomson and Tom Watson have not climbed since.

Here they are on the 2nd tee on the Old Course at St Andrews with Vardon driving off and Braid, ball in hand, apparently next to play. Oddly, Taylor is holding a mashie, a club he certainly would not have used on this hole for his tee shot. The explanation? Taylor had mastery with this club and Flower wanted to show him holding one.

(Left) *'Spy Caricatures', 1890–1910*
'Spy' (Sir Leslie Ward, 1851–1922) produced a series of cartoons – humorous drawings would, perhaps, be a better description – for Vanity Fair *magazine. Reproduced here is almost the full range of his golf drawings. From the top, left to right, they show J.H. Taylor, Horace Hutchinson, H. Mallaby Delley and James Braid, and, below, Robert Maxwell, John Ball, S. Mure Fergusson and Harold (H.H.) Hilton. Though all used in* Vanity Fair *and part of what collectors think of as a set, one – John Ball – is not by 'Spy'. This was drawn by 'Lib' – the Italian Liberio Prosperi – in 1892. It is doubtful whether Ball was much pleased with how he was represented in this rather dejected pose.*

Of the others, it is interesting to note H.H. Hilton's distinctive appearance in the 'Hoylake' cartoon. His features would have been well-known to the magazine's readers. He was seldom seen without a cigarette in his mouth and also usually played in white shoes and stockings.

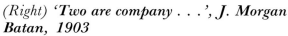

"TWO ARE COMPANY—"

(Right) *'Two are company . . .', J. Morgan Batan, 1903*
The point of this picture is to show that the dog is man's best friend, perhaps followed by the golf club. Although the women's game was growing too, such was the explosion of interest in golf in the early years of the century on both sides of the Atlantic that the concept of, if not the term, golf widow began to develop.

Tom Morris, A.J. Balfour and Graham Murray, c.1903

In the early years of the century, photographs were often printed as postcards, either for personal or commercial use. The first of these shows the British politician, the Rt Hon Arthur Balfour, 'driving himself in' as captain of the Royal and Ancient. It must have been a reasonable shot, as Old Tom Morris (extreme left foreground) is clapping his efforts. Balfour had become Prime Minister in 1902 and the publicity his golfing activities received gave a very considerable boost to the game. President Eisenhower, a poor but enthusiastic player, had a similar effect in the United States much later. However, he was so much photographed on golf courses or with players such as Ben Hogan and Arnold Palmer that people came to feel that he was not giving his full attention to the affairs of the nation. Playing golf was not part of the image cultivated by his successor, J.F. Kennedy.

Silver Statue of F.G. Tait, c.1900

Freddie Tait was the best loved golfer of his time, but his life was cut short when he was killed leading a charge of the Black Watch regiment in 1900 in South Africa during the Boer War. Born in 1870, he had twice won the Amateur Championship, in 1896 and 1898, and lost to the eventual eight-times champion John Ball in 1899. At his best in matchplay (he dismissed strokeplay as mere rifle shooting), Tait would surely have taken more titles. Like his great amateur contemporaries, John Ball and Harold Hilton, he might even have won a British Open, having been third on two occasions – perhaps his dislike of strokeplay got the better of him. This silver figure is one of several representations.

Golfing Types, 1905

More than other sports, golf has often been seen as a humorous subject by artists. Is there something intrinsically ridiculous in the serious way in which grown adults address the problem of hitting a small stationary ball? Or is it just that golf, being one of the few sports that admits conversation during play, has thrown up more than its fair share of 'characters'?

Sunningdale, 1900s
A fine example of what was considered the best in clubhouse architecture. The Old Course at Sunningdale in Ascot, west of London, was designed by Willie Park Junior, and became a fashionable place to play at the turn of the century. Sunningdale was to be the scene of a notable round of 66 by Bobby Jones in the 1920s. His card still hangs in the club's dining room.

VICTOR VENNER.

His Girl, Victor Venner, 1903
*The artist has painted a male golfer out with a young
woman. Gallantly, he carries her golf bag as well
as his own, but he looks to have things other than
golf on his mind.*

The Budget League, 1909
Golf and politics started to mix in the 1890s, and they have become ever closer friends since, especially in the United States. The British politician Lloyd George was a keen golfer, being a member at Walton Heath and other clubs. This cartoon reflects his interest in golf and also the budget he introduced as Chancellor of the Exchequer in 1909, which inflamed the landed classes and was delayed by the House of Lords.

Harry Vardon, 1900
In 1900, Harry Vardon embarked on a long tour of the United States to promote both golf and a guttie ball called the Vardon Flyer. His exhibition matches attracted a great deal of attention, but promotion of the ball did not go nearly so well. The guttie was already doomed by Coburn Haskell's wound ball.

During his trip, Vardon also won the U.S. Open. On his only other entries, in 1913 he tied but lost the play-off, and in 1920 he finished second. At almost 50 years old, he seemed to be heading for victory with a few holes left to play but then dropped shot after shot when a strong wind blew up. This oil portrait was painted during his 1900 tour and is not a good likeness.

(Above) **Harry Vardon**
Harry Vardon pictured at the club, South Herts, where he served until his death in 1937. Note how he allowed his left elbow to flex during the backswing.

(Right) **Sandy Herd, 1911**
Sandy Herd was the first man to win the British Open Championship using the rubber core ball. He won at Hoylake in 1902, shortly after the ball had arrived in Britain from the United States, where Coburn Haskell had invented it before the turn of the century.

He had been offered one to try by the great Hoylake amateur, John Ball, during a practice round and was an immediate convert. Some were not so quick to make up their minds. The old gutta percha ball was easier to use on and around the greens, but in the long game it required better striking and did not run so far.

Herd was famous in his day for a prolonged but rapid waggle before hitting the ball. His success made the golf world realize that the waggle was not an annoying habit, but a good way of loosening up the muscles prior to a shot.

A Golf Song, c. 1900
Popular songs reflect popular interests; by the beginning of the century golf was riding high in the charts.

(Below) **Men's Fashion Plate, c.1905**
An advertisement for what the fashion-conscious man should wear for golf. Jackets are not suitable for golf because their stiffness impedes movement, but they did not really go out until after World War I, when the idea of clothes especially for the sport began to take hold. This plate was produced as a sample for a company representative to carry around.

(Left) **The Christie Girl, 1903**
This painting by G.F. Christie was a watercolour from which a successful postcard was produced. Clothing for women was getting a little less cumbersome, although that skirt would still have been a hazard in high winds or heavy rain.

(Right) *'Caddie Sir', 1903,* and (above) **Three
Cats, 1908, Louis Wain**
*Louis Wain (1860 – 1939) enjoyed a wide
reputation for his pictures of cats. Golf, as we see
here, was one of their pastimes.*

'Try our cork-tipped golf-bag . . .', F.H. Townsend, 1908

The full caption 'Try our cork-tipped golf-bag – IT FLOATS! – and our combination spoon-mashie paddle' tells the story. It seems that the young

caddie is fearful of being next in line after the broken golf club. The cartoon is also a comment on how sophisticated golf equipment had become.

(Left) **Royal Musselburgh Golf Club, 1906**
Though most of the evidence has long disappeared, it used to be the custom to summon the local photographer when anything worthy of record was taking place at a golf club. With the enormous growth of senior golf, however, an event such as this foursome of octogenarians may well be commoner (though maybe still not common enough to pass without a photograph!).

The 6th Green at Romford, The 15th Green at Rye, The 7th Tee at Royal Lytham & St Anne's, and Muirfield, Harry Rountree, 1910
The New Zealander Harry Rountree's paintings of golf courses (here and overleaf) and other golf work are outstanding. The golf course scenes are perpetuated in the book The Golf Courses of the British Isles *by Bernard Darwin, a must for collectors of golf books. However, the descriptive text of a book written in 1910 has now to be largely unrepresentative of the courses as they are today, so for many it is Rountree's paintings that give the book its main appeal. Reproductions of the volume are available in both Britain and the United States. The American version is by far the better.*

Rountree was a landscape painter, as well as a talented line draughtsman, and seems always entranced by the beauty and peace of places where golf is played. Although a keen golfer himself, the players in his paintings are usually subsidiary to the main subject – the landscape.

Note that he seems able to deal equally effectively with landscapes of various kinds from bleak and open to cluttered.

The 6th Green at Romford

The 15th Green at Rye

The 7th Tee at Royal Lytham & St Annes

The 4th and 14th Greens at Muirfield

Ladies at Morris County, Golf, 1910s
Golf grew at an enormous rate in the United States until the Depression. This was reflected by its becoming an ever more popular subject with painters and illustrators. Here we have an Edwardian mixed foursome in New Jersey.

Golfers by a Riverbank, French, 1912
Many painters have had their eye turned by an idyllic golfing scene, painted it and then moved on, leaving no details of themselves or the subject. This anonymous watercolour of two women golfers and a caddie may have been painted at Pau, the oldest club in continental Europe.

Royal County Down, St Andrews, and North Berwick, Michael Brown, 1912

The golfing work of Michael Brown is now highly rated. He produced a series of paintings of golf courses for a promotional calendar issued by the Life Association of Scotland. The beauty of Scottish courses has often been captured by painters, and Brown's work for the Life Association (here and overleaf) rates with the best.

Royal County Down at Newcastle in Northern Ireland, close to the border, is a magnificent test of golf. Perhaps rather more important, it is one of the world's most beautiful courses. The view of St Andrews shows the Old Course. The North Berwick course is on the coast, east of Edinburgh.

(Below) **Royal County Down**

(Left) *St Andrews*

(Below) **North Berwick**

NORTH BERWICK.

Sponsored Golf, F.H. Townsend, 1910
This pen and ink sketch by F.H. Townsend is a comment on both how heavily golf products were advertised and how much golf was used to advertise non-golfing products – even as early as 1910. Sponsorship in the modern sense was also around, with the first sponsored event, the News of the World Tournament, dating from the first years of the 20th century.

OXO Advertisement, 1910
With the growing popularity of golf, quite a few products were promoted as being beneficial for your game, as in this 1910 magazine advertisement for OXO stock cubes. Note the very healthy looking young woman, compared to her antique father. Early advertising latched on to golf for reasons similar to those that motivate much contemporary advertising: the desire to have products associated with good health.

John Ball, 1910

This apparently quite aged gentleman is John Ball, who was born in 1861. He was 49 and on his way to the seventh of his eight wins in the British Amateur. The length of his career as a winner of major championships – from 1888 to 1912 – is most impressive, especially as the opposition was strong. Ball is often given credit for being the first man on long shots to go for the hole, rather than the green.

(Left) Willie Park Junior, 1911
Willie Park Junior was Open Champion in 1887 and 1889. As a golfer pure and simple, he was thought by all to be the greatest of putters and would have swept all before him if his long game had been as good. However, Park used his golfing success to build other careers. First he created a flourishing business both sides of the Atlantic in club manufacture and innovative design. In time, mass production made that less viable, so he then expanded his efforts in golf architecture where, again, he was very prominent in both Britain and the United States.

(Right) Violet Hezlet, 1911
The Irish player, Violet Hezlet, in 1911, when she was runner-up for the British Ladies' Championship. She survived to the age of 99. Her sisters, May and Florence, were also superior golfers; May won the British title three times. The three sisters had an important hand in the setting up of the Curtis Cup, through their friendship with the Curtis sisters.

(Left) **Ladies' Fashion, 1910s**
Is this plate a fantasy of what a woman should wear for golf, or a stunning outfit worn by someone for whom the club is no more than an amusing detail?

(Above) **Cecilia Leitch, 1911**
The women's game took longer to achieve popularity in the United Kingdom than in the United States, although it soon produced its stars. Charlotte Cecilia Pitcairn Leitch, always called 'Cecil', ruled the roost in Britain until the overnight arrival of Joyce Wethered. Despite the palm grips she used, she compiled a splendid championship record, winning the French title five times, the British on four occasions and the English twice.

(Right) **Edwardian Ladies by the Sea, H.E. Harvey, c.1910**
Despite the stiff breeze, this anonymous group is clearly very relaxed.

The Fivesome, B. Turner, 1912
Today, anywhere where golf is played at all seriously, you would be severely admonished if you played in any group larger than four. In the halcyon days when courses were less crowded, etiquette was not so rigidly enforced.

WILLING TO LEARN.

Two Valentine Cards, 1911, 1912
It is difficult to imagine another sport that could have been used to portray romantic interest between the sexes – lawn tennis possibly. The cards may have been fine to send a female golfing sweetheart, but if the player was a man, the sender may well have been ironic. After all, then as now, golf was also known to distract a young man's fancy.

TO MY VALENTINE
Though a Golfing Match is most famous sport,
A much better match it would be
With hands united and true hearts plighted
A Love Match to make with me.

Charles Blair Macdonald, Gari Melchers, after 1910

This painting by Gari Melchers depicts perhaps the United States's greatest golfing pioneer, Charles Blair Macdonald at his finest golf course creation, the National Golf Links, constructed in 1910. It was opened with an invitation tournament which was won by Harold Hilton, a four times winner of the British Amateur and with two British Opens on his record. Hilton remains the only British player to have won the US Amateur, which he did in 1911.

Macdonald had learned his golf while a student at St Andrews University where he played with Young Tom Morris, among others. As golf did not exist in the United States when he returned he had to do without but by 1893 had designed the first 18 hole course in the country.

Later he conceived the idea of producing an ideal golf course. To help him do so, he visited Britain to study features of golf holes that he might want to include. The results of these researches were eventually incorporated into his National at Southampton, Long Island. Wrongly, it is often stated that Macdonald copied entire holes and reproduced them here; what he actually did was admire such features as the placement of a bunker, a demanding drive, the alignment of a green, and so on, and visualize how the terrain he was working with at The National could accommodate them to the best advantage.

When the National was opened, it was regarded, on both sides of the Atlantic, as a major step forward in golf architecture (a term which Macdonald himself invented).

Pit Before 18th Green, Pinehurst, North Carolina, 1920s

Pinehurst in North Carolina is a quiet little place almost entirely devoted to golf, rather like Gullane in East Lothian. James W. Tufts first established it as a winter resort when northern courses were closed before the turn of the century. Gradually more and more courses were built, but the Number 2 was the special delight of Donald Ross, the course architect from Dornoch in Scotland, and he made subtle changes over the years. Pinehurst is not intensely interested in hosting tournaments, but Densmore Shute won the P.G.A. here in 1936 and the United States won the Ryder Cup in 1951. The U.S.P.G.A. Hall of Fame is located in the town.

THE FIRST AGE OF THE PROFESSIONALS

The first professionals in golf were primarily ball and club makers. However, they were not tied entirely to manufacture, as to a limited extent their products were bought as a result of their proven golfing prowess. Their sales were usually local and their income was, of necessity, supplemented by caddying and partnering the local gentry.

The first purely playing professional was Young Tom Morris. He seems never to have made a club or ball or acted as a caddie, but he did partner the gentlemen. That he could be a match and tournament professional, and was allowed across the social barriers, was due to his genius for the game. This had become obvious very early on, no doubt helped by his father's fame. When he won his first Open Championship in 1868, he was still only 17, and to this day remains easily the youngest winner of this or any other major championship. While photographs, paintings and drawings of his father proliferated, especially later in the century, because of his early death few visual records of Young Tom were made. When he had made the original British Open Championship trophy (a fine morocco belt with silver buckle and embellishments) his own by winning three times in a row, he posed in all his pomp in, probably, a St Andrews or Prestwick photographer's studio. Sadly, the photos would soon become the basis of his sculpted tomb in the graveyard of St Andrews Cathedral.

Young Tom's last match was an encounter with the amateur Arthur Molesworth in the snows of November 1875 with the proud fathers caddying for their respective sons. None of the portrayals of him however, tell us much about how Young Tom played the game. All merely depict his open stance, with Tom about to swing. As it is, it is from written accounts that we learn how boldly Young Tom putted and how furiously he swung, so much so that his bonnet was often dislodged. Much later, one man said that he could not imagine anyone ever playing golf better than Young Tom, but we have only his scores and victories as evidence.

After Young Tom's death on Christmas morning 1875, those who came after seemed lesser men. In general, the professionals were neither painted nor photographed during play, although the equipment available to do so was far more sophisticated than many would imagine today. Such champions as Bob Martin and Bob Ferguson have left just a face on the retina of time. Instead, artists showed far more interest in the great amateurs who appeared towards the end of the 19th century – John Ball, Harold Hilton and Freddie Tait. Each won the British Amateur Championship when the title meant as much as the Open, and the first two also took the Open.

For a brief period, it seemed possible for amateurs to be better than professionals, but a great trio was also on the rise: in order of appearance, these were J.H. Taylor, Harry Vardon and James Braid. They established a nearly complete stranglehold on the British Open and were nicknamed 'The Great Triumvirate'. Between the mid-1890s and World War I, they took the title 16 times. Each was dominant in his turn and the greatest of them, Vardon, came back when his best days seemed over.

These three were the biggest names during the first golf explosion. When World War I ended, each was about 50, and there were new names to conjure with, mainly from the other side of the Atlantic. Undoubtedly the greatest of these was the amateur Bobby Jones, the competitor with the best-ever strike rate, the most hypnotically rhythmic of swings, and a steely character to match. By far the most photographed golfer of the 1920s, his face appeared everywhere. He was, after all, not just the greatest of golfers but the greatest sportsman of his era.

His closest rival was another American, Water Hagen. He once thrashed Jones in a challenge match when his putter was working well, but never won a major title when Jones was in the field. Hagen's appeal was very different. Jones was the Southern straight-shooter gentleman, ever the 'parfait gentil knight', admired, even venerated wherever he went; Hagen was simply the most enjoyable character golf has produced. He was little painted for, they said, his swing

British Open Champions, 1928 or 1929

A meeting of generations. The American, Walter Hagen (second from left, front row), first won the British Open in 1922, three years after his last U.S. Open win. Here he poses following his win in 1928 or 1929 with other Open champions from previous years. They are (back row) Harry Vardon, James Braid, Sandy Herd, Jack White and Arnaud Massy (winners from 1896 to 1916). In the front are George Duncan (winner in 1920), Hagen himself, Jim Barnes (1925) and Ted Ray (1912). The dapper Hagen stands out as the dominant figure!

Walter Hagen was not the first player to cross the Atlantic Ocean purely and simply to play competitive golf; the years that followed World War I saw both American and British players starting to compete regularly at courses on each other's home territory.

began with a sway and ended with a lurch, neither of them elegant qualities. But what a deft touch the man had once he neared the green! He inspired cartoonists more than painters, and enchanted all with his game.

Despite the Wall Street Crash and a worldwide slump, the fairly expensive game of golf kept going, although some grandiose clubhouse and course-building projects collapsed. People were playing in their millions and popular art reflected this.

Golfing holidays, for example, had just as great an appeal as today, even if they were too expensive for the working man. The resorts of the United States, Britain and Europe exhorted all to come, and the railways were eager carriers. As a result, the best posters come from this period.

At the same time advertisers realized that linking products with a popular game played by some of the more affluent members of society could only improve sales, and magazines learnt quickly that a golfing scene on the front cover was a sure bet to attract readers.

Ease of travel benefited professional players too. As air travel became lower priced, more comfortable, and fast, crossing the Atlantic or the United States to play a tournament became less of an expedition. The great players of the day became faces, not just names, to a wide public in Britain and North America, and their earnings rose correspondingly.

J.H. Taylor, c.1920

This photograph of J.H. Taylor in action with, probably, a Braid-Mills putter was taken after World War I. Taylor is gallantly playing it up for the camera, pretending anxiety over the fate of his putt. If Vardon was definitely the worst putter of the Great Triumvirate, Taylor was probably the best.

Although by now past his best, Taylor played competitive golf long enough to be included in the team for the first of that continuing series of United States v. Great Britain matches, in 1921, which became the Ryder Cup.

Golfers Magazine, *1915*

A striking demonstration of just how stylish a game golf had become by 1915. The two golfers, lady and gentleman, are both impeccably dressed, and what may well be a fine new clubhouse in the classical style is half-hidden in the distance.

Chick Evans, one of the magazine's two editors, was a great amateur from Indianapolis whose finest hours came in 1916 when he led the U.S. Open all the way, his 286 setting a record which stood for 20 years. He achieved this with only seven clubs: brassie, spoon, jigger, mid-iron, lofter, niblick and putter. The same year Evans also won the U.S. Amateur, becoming the first man to take both titles the same year. Apart from Bobby Jones (who else?), he is the only man to do so.

***Portmarnock (Coming Back From Golf),
Harry Rountree, 1910***
*At Portmarnock on the Irish coast near Dublin,
golfers used to have to cross to the course by sailing
boat or, in this manner, at low (or not so low) tide.
The course today is one of the greatest in Ireland,
entirely fit to host an Open. It has, in fact, been
visited by the British Amateur Championship (in
1949), the only time the event has been played on
what is technically foreign soil. In reality, Irish
golf and British golf are largely unified, despite the
political upheavals involving the two countries.*

Portmarnock, Harry Rountree, 1910
Both Portmarnock paintings are from Darwin's celebrated book on British golf courses. This painting shows golfers about to play to the final green.

Four Golfers, Roga, 1913
These four studies are more to do with character and clothing than the game of golf. It is noticeable that the artist completely failed to handle the 'technical drawing' of the clubs. All the same, the studies would have found a good sale among the growing numbers of golfers keen to adorn their walls with scenes of the sport.

The First International Foursome, Alan Stewart, 1919

Do not be deceived by the clothing, for this painting was not produced until 1919. It depicts a match played in 1682 when the future King James II, partnered by the best local player he could find, a certain John Patersone (a 'poor shoemaker'), won what is sometimes called 'The First International Foursome' as they were playing some English aristocrats. The game arose out of an argument over the origins of the game, which they decided to settle by playing rather than by discussion. The match was played over Leith Links near Edinburgh, and the painting now hangs in the headquarters of the United States Golf Association at Far Hills, New Jersey.

The painting is another example of the desire of golf enthusiasts in the early years of this century to make up for the paucity of historical records.

"'Tis best to be off with the old love before you are on with the new."

Cartoon, G.W.P., c.1915

Why on earth is the new girlfriend depicted with a golf bag and fashionable smart dress in this otherwise pastoral scene? The reason can only be that golf tended to be associated with the smart ways of city sophisticates, who were likely to take advantage of those with rather simpler country ways. 'The best to be off with the old love before you are on with the new,' runs the cartoon's caption, and it is surely indicative that it is the new love who carries the clubs.

Collier's magazine, cover, 1916
This cover of Collier's *magazine depicts the frustrations of playing golf badly − all the worse if the weather is hot and there is rather too much weight to carry around the golf course. As the magazine was a general interest one, and not a specialist golf publication, the decision to lead with a golf story and illustration testifies to the selling power the sport had already achieved.*

(Left) **George Duncan being Awarded the British Open Trophy, 1920**

In the 1920 British Open at Royal Cinque Ports, Deal, George Duncan began with a pair of 80s. He was a long way behind Abe Mitchell's start of 74, 73. However, wandering about the Open Exhibition, Duncan came upon a new driver he liked the feel of. The next day, the play of both golfers was transformed. In the morning, Mitchell staggered in with an 84 to Duncan's 71, and his lead was gone. In the afternoon, Duncan's 72 brought him home for his only championship victory.

(Right) **Joyce Wethered, Charles Ambrose, 1920**

Joyce Wethered has often been called the greatest woman golfer of all time, although the competition in the women's game today, especially in the United States, is surely tougher than she faced. Both Henry Cotton and Bobby Jones considered she was the best player around at the time, male or female (while making allowance for length of drive).

Her record in the British Ladies' Championship was superb. She lost the 1921 final to Cecil Leitch, but won in 1922, 1924 and 1925. Then, not enjoying competitive golf, she retired until 1929, when she took part again because the event was being held over the Old Course at St Andrews. Once again, she took the title, beating the great American Glenna Collett in the final. Joyce Wethered did not enter again, having won 36 of the 38 matches she ever played in the event. During the Depression she played professionally for a while by taking part in an exhibition series in the United States, and broke many course records during the tour.

"JOYCE"
The Lady Golfer of the Year

By Charles Ambrose

JUNE 16.1921

Life

PRICE 15 CENTS

Golf Number

(Left) **The Wearing of the Green, Life, 1921**
This elegant young woman from the cover of Life *magazine seems to be leaving the 17th green to play her tee shot on the final hole without first replacing the flag. This is a heinous crime — but perhaps there is a caddie or doting young man out of the picture to do it for her.*

(Right) **Golfers, George Biddle, 1924**
The painter George Biddle conveys an unusual feeling of golf. The woman in the foreground, despite having her dogs with her (very often not allowed), does not appear to be having an enjoyable day. Her clothes cling curiously in a very 1920s fashion, as they do to the svelte figure with the odd grip and impossible swing in the middle distance. Biddle has carefully avoided too great a realism, and demonstrates that by the 1920s golf had become sufficiently established to be the subject of art that was concerned with more than just depicting the game and its locations.

(Overleaf) *A Drive, Bunkered, Putting, A Bad Lie, John Hassall, 1920s*
In the first of these four watercolours the caddie is obviously impressed by the length of the woman's drive. In the next, the very plugged bunker lie is going to cause problems. In the third we have a golfer who is not in the least confident about holing out the last from a very short distance indeed. Behind, we could assume, is his daughter, and the match could rest on this putt. In the fourth, the golfer is caught in the rough. He has the rapt attention of his family, who may well be wishing they were on the beach rather than in the dunes.

A DRIVE

BUNKERED

PUTTING

A BAD LIE

WALTER HAGEN.

GENE SARAZEN.

Cigarette Cards: Molly Gourlay, Gene Sarazen, Walter Hagen, Sam Snead, 1920s-40s

Churchman's of Ipswich produced several series of golfing cigarette cards in Britain in the 1920s and 1930s, although the earlier cards of golf players date back to the 1890s. Walter Hagen was at the peak of his fame in the 1920s, his career culminating in his fourth and last British Open title at Muirfield in 1929. He broke the course record and also played superbly on the final day's 36 holes in rough weather. Hagen also won two U.S. Opens and five U.S. P.G.A. titles when the event was played as matchplay. This last feat means that Hagen can be considered the greatest ever at this form of golf; he even managed to crush the great Bobby Jones, with whom he could very seldom cope in strokeplay championships.

Gene Sarazen always stood just a little in Hagen's shadow, yet his record was very fine. Born in 1902, he was U.S. Open champion by 1922, and won the P.G.A. both that year and the next. Perhaps because of a very unorthodox grip, his career then went into decline for some years, and although he was able to win tournaments, he could not secure the majors. Then in the early 1930s he regained form. 1932 was his greatest year, when he dominated the British Open from start to finish, and then went home to win the U.S. Open as well, finishing with a 66 to do so. Although Sarazen won the P.G.A. three times, his most memorable feat came in the Masters in 1935. Craig Wood, already in the clubhouse, seemed to have the title in his pocket. Sarazen was on the 15th, a par 5, needing a three birdie finish to tie. He rode into his second shot with a 4 wood and holed out for a double eagle. With that stroke he had caught Wood, and he then played out the remaining holes in par and won the play-off the next day.

Molly Gourlay was at her peak from the mid-1920s to the mid-1930s, winning the French Ladies' title three times and the English once. She played in two Curtis Cup teams and when she decided to give up golf at the age of 73, she still had a 4 handicap.

Sam Snead will go down in golfing history as the greatest American player to fail to win his national Open. Once he threw it away with an 8 on the final hole, and another time missed a short putt on the last hole of the 18 hole play-off with Lew Worsham. No one, however, has come close to his record 84 wins on the U.S. Tour. If he had been playing for the sums of money on offer today, he would surely have amassed something like $15 - $20 million.

Snead was the first very long driver also to have an excellent allround game, with his wedge and sand iron play being just as outstanding. However, on the greens he eventually had his troubles with the short putts. In desperation, he decided to putt croquet-style between his legs, and when the golf authorities banned that, adapted his method to face the hole chest on and putt from outside his right foot. One can wonder what Sam thinks of today's long putters jammed into chin and chest, which have not been banned at the time of writing.

If the U.S. Open eluded Snead, he had less difficulty with the other majors, winning the British Open at his only serious attempt in 1946, and both the P.G.A. and Masters three times.

CHURCHMAN'S CIGARETTES

MISS MOLLY GOURLAY

SAM SNEAD
PROFESSIONAL GOLF STAR

(Left) **Walter Hagen, 1922**

Walter Hagen photographed in 1922, the year he won his first British Open title, at Royal St George's, Sandwich. Hagen was always a dapper dresser, as here in his bow tie. He is also often credited with introducing two-tone shoes for golf.

Besides his two U.S. Opens (in 1914 and 1919), he won the U.S. P.G.A. five times, winning four in a row, from 1924 to 1927. No one before or since has matched this feat in any major tournament.

His British wins were, perhaps, inspired by his reaction to the snobbery then rife in the game in the United Kingdom. He arrived at Royal St George's in 1922 to find that professionals were not allowed to change or eat in the clubhouse. His response was to hire a limousine, park it in front of the forbidden clubhouse, and use it as his base. When he went on to win, he gave the cheque to his caddie in disgust at the derisory sum.

(Below) **Walter Hagen at Muirfield, 1929**

Walter Hagen awaits the presentation of the British Open trophy at Muirfield in 1929. It was, perhaps, his greatest performance and his fourth and final victory. However, if you had asked Hagen about it in later years, you would have found him casual enough not to remember the wheres, whens and how manys.

(Left) **Haig Clubs, 1928**
Walter Hagen became involved in club manufacture towards the end of his great years. In these two advertisements, he is putting the case for a 'uniform' set of clubs — what would later be called a matched set. Hagen was very much an instinct player, and not especially attached to particular clubs, but the idea of having an array of clubs supposedly identical in feel though different in length was innovative and became a standard most club golfers were to adhere to. Many professionals today, however, play with a totally unmatched set. They prefer to alter the lofts and lies and stick lead tape to them until they get a feel in individual clubs that they like. If they are great names in the game and have a sponsoring company, their every whim will be met, rather as in Grand Prix motor racing.

Haig Ultra clubs sold well for many years, although Hagen himself soon lost interest in the project, no doubt content with his annual fee or royalty. However, after a gap of many years, he did once visit the factory and was soon demonstrating to craftsmen where they were going wrong.

(Above) **Mr and Mrs Walter Hagen, 1924**
A keen party-goer, Hagen was not married long. There are many pictures of Hagen with women, but this one is with his wife, just after he had won his second British Open at Hoylake in 1924.

(Left) **Pleasant Memories of My Fourth British Open, Walter Hagen, 1929**
Did Walter Hagen start the custom of signing letters 'Golfingly yours', which is still followed today? Judging by the vast crowd Hagen is probably putting out on the final green.

GOLF

Il n'arrive jamais à mettre dans le trou.

Aquarelle de Jaquelux

Le Sourire, magazine cover, 1925
Putting has always been the mystery that cannot be solved — except for a brief spell. The French clearly have the same problem — 'It never goes into the hole'.

'The Man who Played Four off the First Tee',
H.H. Harris, 1928
As seen in this picture from Golf Illustrated, one
person's delay has long caused irritation to fellow
golfers. Such a sentiment is evidence of the increasing
call on courses; with more people using them, the
leisure to be incompetent vanishes.

Golfing Lady, Sem, 1920s

It seems likely that this gouache by the French artist Sem was intended for a holiday poster. This is partly suggested by the umbrella-shaded male figure in the background, and partly by its similarity to much of the poster art of the period. It was, almost certainly, not intended to be realistic. As things stand, the lady has played an air shot, and both her stance and leg action were by no means exemplary. Golf's commercial pull was such that it was considered a subject for poster art, but the artist is here more concerned with graphic effect than with pleasing golf purists.

(Right) Advertisement, Life, 1924

An advertisement for golf in Bermuda in Life *magazine in January 1924. Far more courses closed down in the winter in the United States than in Britain, but keen golfers had the money available to set out in search of golf in the sun. Bermuda had to compete for their custom against Florida and other southern states.*

(Below) 'George', Stanley R. Flint, 1920s

Personalities have always featured in every club even if, as with this otherwise anonymous 'George', their local fame is not transformed into lasting celebrity.

BERMUDA FOR GOLF

Enjoy Bermuda's flawless greens, where 18 holes are 18 tropical pictures, where the fascination of the scenery vies with the perfection of the courses.

The Bermuda Amateur Championship Golf Tournament will be played at Riddell's Bay, week of January 14.

The winter climate, 60° to 70°, permits every outdoor sport—golf, tennis, sailing, surf bathing, fishing, riding, driving, cycling, horse racing. No automobiles, street cars, railroads—an ideal place for rest, recreation, and sightseeing. Modern hotels, boarding houses, cottages, with a wide range of rates.

Steamships sail every few days. Only 48 hours from New York. No passports required. Request illustrated booklet from The Royal Mail Steam Packet Company, 26 Broadway, Furness Bermuda Line, 34 Whitehall Street, New York, any travel bureau, or

The Bermuda Trade Development Board
141 West 36th Street, New York
(A Department of the Bermuda Government, which has authorized the publication of this advertisement)

(Far left) **French Golf Course, 1924**
Golf has always tended to be for the chic few in France, as reflected in this 1924 painting. This has changed a little in recent years, both in France and elsewhere on the Continent. As a result, France has started to produce more international competitors. Arnaud Massy, in 1907 the first non-Briton to win the British Open, may yet be challenged for the title of France's greatest golfer ever.

(Left) **Royal St Davids, C.T. Abell, c.1930**
No other course is quite so dominated by a castle – in this instance, Harlech, built during the conquest of Wales by Edward I. It would be delightful if Wales could join Scotland and England as a country holding the British Open, but it is unlikely ever to happen. If it did, Royal St Davids would receive close consideration.

Bobby Jones, Chicago Sunday Tribune, 1928
No one in the history of golf has bettered Bobby Jones in his strike rate of winning major championships. Before he retired at the age of 28, he played only about 50 tournaments in all and won about half of them. Thirteen were major championships, a record which no-one approached until Jack Nicklaus bettered it – though over a much greater period of time. Jones, for instance, won three of the four British Opens he entered.

He was the last amateur to dominate the game, and as an amateur, his golf year was very different from his mainly professional contemporaries. Most of his golf was confined to his home golf club – and then off he would go to win the U.S. Open or Amateur. His competitive career in Britain was even more limited because of lack of funds, and was mainly confined to years when the U.S. Walker Cup team was over. Having failed to win the British Amateur in one such year – 1926 – he decided to stay on for the Open – and won. He then felt that he ought to defend his title and won again at St Andrews. Jones could not, however, spare the time in either 1928 or 1929, but in 1930 he set his sights on the apparently impossible Grand Slam of the Open and Amateur titles both sides of the Atlantic. That accomplished, he felt there were no more worlds to conquer and retired.

He remained intensely interested in golf, however, and was involved in making instructional films, helping design Augusta National with Alister Mackenzie, and starting off the Augusta National Invitational, now know as the Masters – a title preferred by some but viewed with distaste by Jones as being too grandiose. He went on to become the first golf writer of excellence who had also been a great player.

(Above) **Bobby Jones, 1926**
Bobby Jones taken after he had won the British Open of 1926 at Royal Lytham & St Anne's. One of the shots he played in doing this has gone down into golfing folklore. One behind his playing partner, Al Watrous, playing the 71st hole, Jones got too much draw on his ball, while Watrous was perfectly placed along the right. Jones then nipped his ball perfectly from a sandy lie with a 4 iron and found the green. 'There goes $100,000,' said Watrous, and later three-putted this 17th green. (£50 was the first prize for a professional winner, such as Watrous, but the kudos, then as now, brought the money rolling in.)

(Below) **Bobby Jones at St Andrews, 1936**
While on his way to watch the 1936 Olympic Games in Berlin, Jones stopped off at Gleneagles Hotel. Being quite near St Andrews, he could not resist the opportunity of revisiting the scene of two of his championship victories and playing the Old Course once more. The news of his visit spread quickly, and this is the crowd which had gathered by the time Jones drove off at the 1st.

Although it was a casual, non-competitive round, Jones was inspired to play brilliantly.

THE SATURDAY EVENING POST

Fashion Advertisement, Saturday Evening Post, 1929

'They tee off the season's style in haberdashery.'

By the end of the 1920s, as this advertisement for Wilson Brothers Haberdashery shows, women's styles on the golf course had changed considerably and had become a lot more practical. We need not assume, however, that the men would be playing in jackets. They are near the clubhouse and a lesson on how to play golf is in progress.

Men's Fashion Plate, 1920s
As golf became fashionable, the clothing market developed to cater for those who wanted to play the game. The fashions displayed would have certainly guaranteed that a golfer looked stylish, but to the modern eye they look less than comfortable. Around the clubhouses of the 1920s (and later) it was as important to look right as to play well.

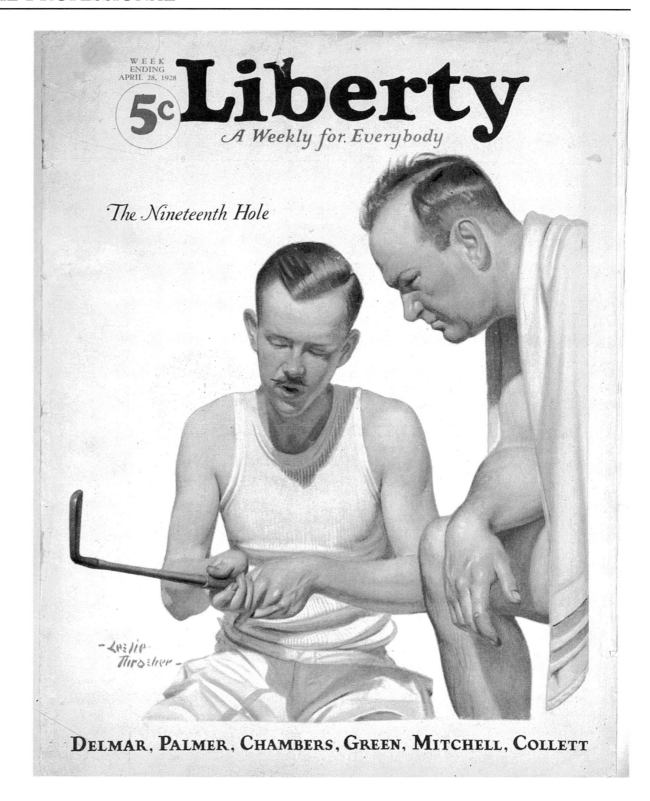

Liberty, magazine cover, 1928
When the round is over, talk in locker room and bar sometimes turns to golf technique. Is, for instance, the interlocking grip superior to the Vardon overlap?

A Golf Course, W. Heath Robinson, 1920s

Heath Robinson is a name that has passed into the English language as a result of the absurd mechanical contrivances he delighted in inventing in his cartoons. Sometimes he turned his attention to golf, to high comic effect, as in this design that appeared on a biscuit tin. The non-stymie double hole must have brought a wry smile to the face of many a golfer in the days when the stymie was still very much a part of the game.

(Above) **Spring Cleaning of Golf Course, W. Heath Robinson, 1920s, and** (right) **cartoons from 'Adventures at Golf', H.M. Bateman, 1922**

The English cartoonists, Bateman and Heath Robinson, were both popular throughout their careers for a variety of humorous work. Bateman was himself a keen golfer.

Heath Robinson's Spring Cleaning *parodies the labour that could go into preparing for the season. Bateman on the other hand reminds us that however splendid a golfer's approach play, all can be ruined by a failure to down that final putt.*

THE PRACTICE SWINGS   THE SCREAMING DRIVE

THE THUNDERING BRASSIE   THE LONG RAKING IRON   THE DELIGHTFUL MASHIE CHIP

THAT—   LITTLE—

TINY—   PUTT!

'Your Tee is Ready, Sir', H.M. Bateman 1933

Bateman's conscientious caddie from The Illustrated London News *thinks that a golf tee should no more be left to go cold than the similar-sounding beverage. Golf cartoons can tell us much about the social relationships of the time.*

(Right) **Railway Poster, 1910s**

Before the days of mass car ownership, the railways in Britain were very keen to encourage golfers to travel by train. Here, the Caledonian Railway lists the golfing attractions on its routes. Some golf and hotel developments, such as Turnberry early in the century and Gleneagles after World War I, were built partly to boost use of the routes on which they lay.

The railways had an enormous influence on the growth of golf in other ways. They enabled members to play at clubs just a few miles away, while other clubs, such as Royal St George's at Sandwich, were started mainly for and by week-ending Londoners. Courses, such as North Berwick near Edinburgh and Dornoch in the far north-east of Scotland, that had already been in existence for a long time, came within reach of golfers taking long summer holidays.

Golf started to expand in the United States later than in Britain. This coincided more closely with the age of mass car-ownership, which, in any case, began earlier than in Europe. The railway was accordingly less important in making away visits to golf courses more popular. The exception in the United States was long-distance travel: winter courses in Florida were brought within reach of the cities of the north-east and the mid-west by the efficient rail network of the first decades of the 20th century.

(Far right) **Teeing off at St Andrews, 1933**

The 1920s and 1930s were, arguably, the golden decades for commercial posters of all kinds. Not a few encouraged golfers to sample the delights of the game, as the railways made playing golf away from home more accessible. Here Michard tries to promote the delights of St Andrews as a golfing centre, with the aim of furthering the use of the London and North Eastern Railway.

THE GOLFING GIRL

"WELL OUT" ON THE TRUE LINE

THE GOLFING GIRL AND ALL HER FRIENDS PLAY GOOD GOLF ON ALL THE GOLF COURSES OF THE DELIGHTFUL DISTRICTS SERVED BY

THE CALEDONIAN RAILWAY

Such As					
ABERDEEN	BLAIRGOWRIE	DAVIDSON'S MAINS	JUNIPER GREEN	MOFFAT	ST FILLANS
ABINGTON	BRIDGE of ALLAN	DUNBLANE	KINGSKNOWE	MONIFIETH	SALTCOATS
ALYTH	CALLANDER	DUNOON	KIRRIEMUIR	MONTROSE	STIRLING
ARBROATH	CARLUKE	EAST KILBRIDE	LANARK	OBAN	STONEHAVEN
AUCHTERARDER	CARNOUSTIE	EDZELL	LAURENCEKIRK	PEEBLES	STRATHAVEN
BARNTON	COMRIE	FORFAR	LOCH AWE	PERTH	UPLAWMOOR
BIGGAR	CRAWFORD	GOUROCK	MACHRIHANISH	ROBERTON	WEMYSS BAY
BISHOPTON	CRIEFF	IRVINE	MILLPORT	ROTHESAY	WHITECRAIGS

ST. ANDREWS

THE HOME OF THE
ROYAL AND ANCIENT
GAME

ILLUSTRATED GUIDE FREE FROM TOWN CLERK OR ANY L·N·E·R OFFICE OR AGENCY

GREAT EASTERN RAILWAY

THE EAST COAST.
IDEAL FOR GOLFING.

(Left) Railway Poster, John Hassall, 1920s
Again a railway poster points out the attractions of a golfing area, rather vaguely designated as the East Coast of England, to which, of course, you should travel by the Great Eastern Railway. The graphic artists employed to produce posters for the railway companies were among the best of their time.

(Right) Car Brochure, 1930s
Though railways greatly helped the spread of golf, their influence began to lessen during the 1930s when car ownership, both sides of the Atlantic, grew. The makers of this Vauxhall car clearly thought that golf-playing created exactly the right image for the purchasers of their new model. The elegance of the lady and gentleman golfers' attire is meant to parallel the assumed elegance of the latest Vauxhall model.

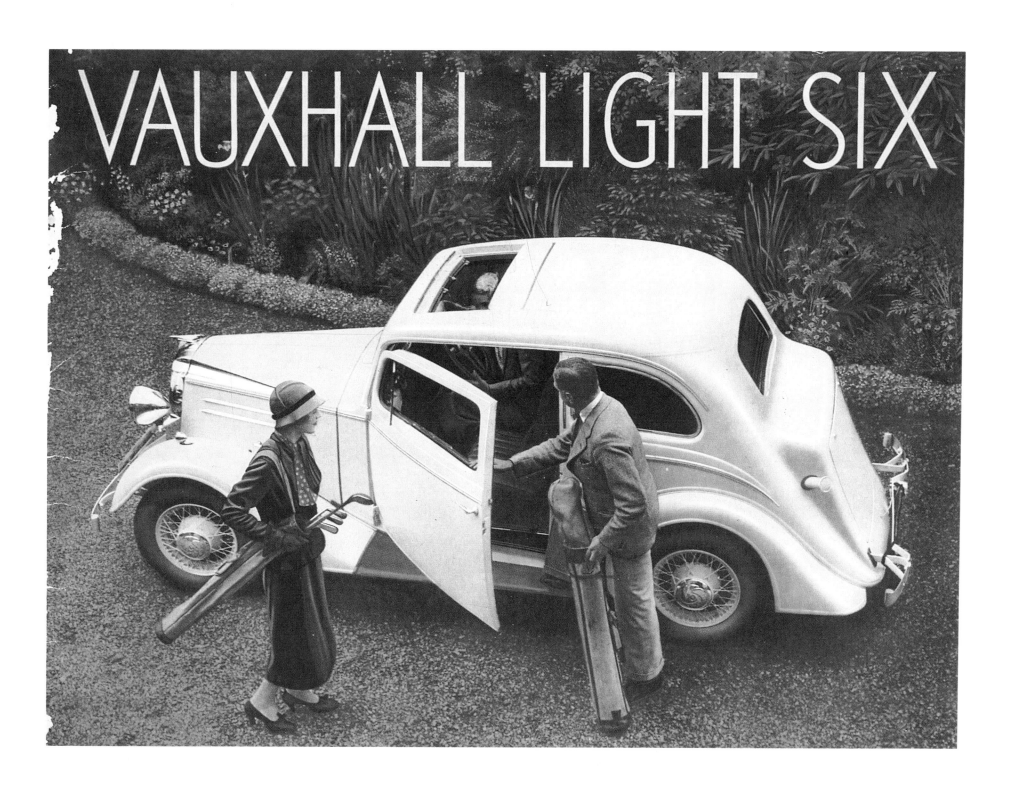

Golf, Lepas, 1930s
This Art Deco poster is not trying to sell anything, but the artist has been captivated by the elegance and energy of the golf swing.

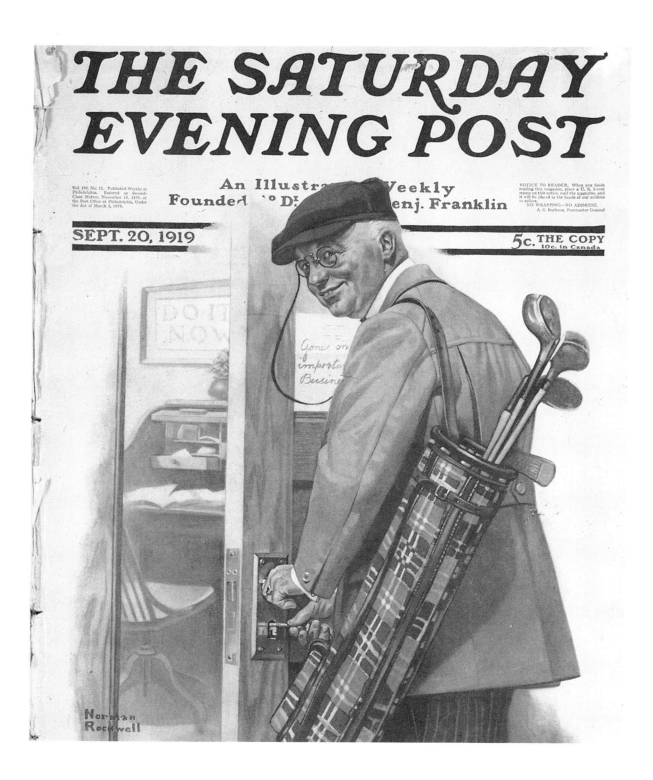

Saturday Evening Post, magazine cover, Norman Rockwell, 1919

The celebrated American magazine illustrator Norman Rockwell (1894–1978) tackled the subject of golf only a few times. Here a businessman seems to be sneaking off early from work (we can see part of the message he is leaving behind).

Clearly, by 1919, and with golf only established in the United States for three decades, the readers of the mass-circulation Saturday Evening Post *had already become well-used to the idea of business on the golf course.*

Life, Sports Number, magazine cover, L.J. Holton, 1927

A brief caption and a wonderfully executed expression of glee on the faces of both truant father and filial caddie say it all: 'The Sport of Missing Men'. The editor of Life evidently thought it a grave enough problem to devote a whole issue to it! In providing an excuse for husbands, and sometimes their sons too, to escape the family home, golf has had a profound (and as yet unresearched) influence on 20th century life.

Good Housekeeping, magazine cover, Jessie Wilcox Smith, 1928
Jessie Wilcox Smith was one of the most popular and financially successful women artists in the United States in the inter-war years. Her work appeared, as here, on the cover of Good Housekeeping *from 1918 to 1935. Her speciality was children, like this angelic-looking boy addressing the ball.*

(Right) **Pictorial Review – Dolly Dingle, Tommy, and the Story of Kittie Cutie, Grace G. Drayton, 1922**
The passion for golf in America in the 1920s spread into children's literature. This story and cut-out is from Pictorial Review. *The message is a simple one – don't forget your breakfast before starting out on a game!*

(Far right) **The Champion, Chloe Preston, 1920s**
Intended to portray a doughty little boy, with an apparently apprehensive caddie, this illustration is evidence of how quickly sentimental art, and indeed children, became associated with golf. Quite simply, golf obsessed the nation at all levels. We also — an interesting detail — see a sand tee still in use.

Pictorial Review for May, 1922

Dolly Dingle, Tommy, and The Story of Kittie Cutie
Drawings by GRACE G. DRAYTON

Oh my ears and whiskers!

it's
GUINNESS TIME

With apologies to Lewis Carroll and Sir John Tenniel

GUINNESS IS GOOD FOR YOUR GOLF

Advertisement, 1932
Guinness was always good for your golf – or anything else – according to the legions of fans of the Irish stout. The advertisers have not only hijacked Lewis Carroll's white rabbit, but have made him a golfer, against all the evidence. Of course Carroll would never have thought of golf as one of those strange examples of adult behaviour that he introduced into the two Alice books!

The Winning Putt, c.1930
Golf has often been popular with advertisers because it is assumed that it is played by people with high incomes. Here, Cadillac associated itself with the game by publishing this picture, although the nearest car must be out of sight by the clubhouse.

CORNELL

MURAD CIGARETTES, FACTORY N° 7 - 3ᴿᴰ DIST N.Y.

WEST POINT

MURAD CIGARETTES, FACTORY N° 7 - 3ᴿᴰ DIST N.Y.

(Left) **Cigarette Cards, 1930s**
It has only recently become questionable to associate sport and cigarette smoking. These cards show Cornell and West Pointers in team uniforms, setting a good example to the nation's youth.

(Right) **Henry Cotton, 1946**
In 1934 Henry Cotton broke a continuous run of American successes in the British Open, which had begun with Arthur Havers' winning in 1923. Cotton went one better in 1937, when he won against a stronger United States entry – the whole Ryder Cup team was in the field. This victory put a shine on his reputation and, although other British players won in the later 1930s, he was the only one to do it twice. With his many other successes, Cotton was thought supreme and, for a time, his second success in foul weather at Carnoustie made some think him the world's best player. The great U.S. stars of the 1920s and early 1930s were in decline or had retired, and Byron Nelson, Sam Snead and Ben Hogan had not yet fully established themselves.

The war interrupted Cotton's career, and he was nearing 40 when it ended. Even so, as this magazine cover reflects, his reputation was as high as ever in 1946. But American Sam Snead won that first post-war Open at St Andrews, and Cotton had to wait until Muirfield in 1948 to win his third title. He was content with that and did not enter again until he was of an age when he was no longer expected to win. Until the performances of Nick Faldo in recent years, Cotton was undoubtedly the greatest British golfer since the days of the Great Triumvirate.

Henry Cotton, 1934
Henry Cotton pictured after his first Open championship victory at Royal St George's, Cotton's start of 67, 65 has still not been bettered, although it was equalled by both Nick Faldo and Greg Norman at St Andrews in 1990.

(Below) **Luffness, Frank W. Wood, 1933, and** *(bottom)* **1st Green at Gullane, Frank W. Wood, 1934**

There are no sheep on major golf courses today, but they – and rabbits – were essential for keeping the grass short and ensuring that golf was playable before mowers gradually came into use in the late 19th century. Even then, they persisted until the

1930s, even on some of the top courses. In Britain, golf was often played on common land or on land rented for a token sum from the local landowner. In either case, sheep and sometimes cattle remained part of the scene, to the great advantage of painters out to capture the romantic beauty of the landscape.

'Those Who Beat Us', Frank Reynolds, 1930s

'To begin with I do object to my oponent (sic) not having a caddie and I can't stand waiting while he potters about. I loathe looking for his ball and I hate a man in a red coat. He got me hopping mad and then!!!'

Thus ran the caption to this cartoon, which is characteristic of the work of Frank Reynolds (1876–1953), one of the best-known cartoonists of his generation. He did a considerable amount of work for Punch and also illustrated an edition of David Copperfield. The book published under the title of The Frank Reynolds' Golf Book well represents the body of his golf work.

Familiar Phrases, Royal & Ancient with Replies Up-to-Date

Phrase — I only hope I shall be able to give you a game
Reply — I doubt it!

I haven't touched a club for a month — you'll knock my head off
I mean to!

Look at this old chap — right in a heel mark!
Serve you — well right!

Oh! Hard Luck! old chap — That bunker ought never to be there
LIAR!

**'Familiar Phrases, with Replies Up-to-date',
Frank Reynolds, 1930s**

*Frank Reynolds, it would seem, had a keen
understanding of the golfing mind! Beneath the
gentlemanly exterior golf can be a highly competitive
game.*

Small Boy (walking round with his father): 'DADDY, HERE'S A BALL FOR YOU.'
Father: 'WHERE DID YOU GET THAT FROM?'
Small Boy: 'IT'S A LOST BALL, DADDY.'
Father: 'ARE YOU SURE IT'S A LOST BALL?'
Small Boy: 'YES, DADDY; THEY'RE STILL LOOKING FOR IT.'

Cartoon, Frank Reynolds, 1920s
*Small boy (walking with his father): 'Daddy, here's
a ball for you.'*
Father: 'Where did you get that from?'
Small boy: 'It's a lost ball, Daddy.'
Father: 'Are you sure it's a lost ball?'
Small boy: 'Yes, Daddy, they're still looking for it.'
   An example of Reynolds' work for Punch. *Golf
jokes — suffiently abundant these days to make a
sizeable compendium — have stuck over the years
to a few familiar themes.*

Lady Golfer, M.S.W., c.1935
It is not clear whether the large numbers of paintings of pretty girls swinging golf clubs were intended for female golfers or whether they were to be bought by men. If the latter, they provided an opportunity to have an image of an attractive woman under the pretext that it was acquired to show the sport. Certainly the golf is often depicted inaccurately; the club head here is not quite right and the girl has let go of the club.

(Left) **Our Trade Golfing Society, Harry Rountree, 1930s**
Harry Rountree (1880-1950) was an all-round golf artist. This was very probably a drawing done to amuse the members of a golf society to which he belonged. There was at least one very wealthy member there whose golf produced numbers as high as his bank balance. His putting style is clearly derived from that pioneered by Sam Snead (see page 137) before it was outlawed.

(Right) **Irate Colonel, H.M. Bateman, 1930s**
Angry golfers have often been the subject of cartoons. Here, H.M. Bateman captures to great effect that irate figure, the red-faced retired military gentleman. Having played a deplorable shot, our subject is kicking his bag to bits. (He would have thrown it into a lake had one been available.) All players know how he feels.

His opponent stands by complacently, while the two caddies are highly amused.

(Right) **Letter by H.M. Bateman, 1930**
A keen golfer who was also a great draughtsman, H.M. Bateman clearly thought nothing of casually appending a little golf scene to a personal letter.

(Left) **Le Golf, Norman Parkinson, 1939**
It is unlikely that Norman Parkinson, the doyen of fashion photographers who died in 1990, was interested to any great extent in golf. At Le Touquet in 1939 the golf was certainly subsidiary to the fashion content, but this photograph captures perfectly the essence of a bunker shot.

(Below) *Golfing Couple, Fougasse, 1930s*
The cartoonist, Fougasse, who is best remembered for his wartime propaganda, here touches on the theme that men think women do not know the object of golf. We can speculate that, very unwillingly, a husband has taken his wife along to the club for her first attempt at the game, for which her choice of clothing looks highly unsuitable. Perhaps he has just explained to her the principles of the golf swing and where she should aim her shot, but he has not succeeded in getting his message through to her.

"I see ... and then you go after it and hit it back?"

THE MODERN GAME

The professional era has been an era of American domination. That domination began before World War II, when amateurs still competed at the top level, but since then the sport has belonged to the professionals – and mainly to Americans. As with Jones, Hagen and Sarazen in the two decades before the war, the names that ring out from the 1940s to the 1980s are almost entirely from the United States: Nelson, Hogan, Snead, Palmer, Nicklaus. Despite that brief comet, Tony Jacklin, and the achievements of the South Africans, Bobby Locke and Gary Player, and the Australian, Peter Thomson, the United States always knew that it had the greatest players of the day. Henry Cotton may have been the greatest British golfer of his day, but he competed very little in the United States, and then without real success.

It took a Spaniard from the Bay of Santander to inspire the Europeans. Sandy Lyle, Nick Faldo, Ian Woosnam and José-Maria Olazabal have all been much encouraged by his example. And any player of excellence playing the European Tour knows that if he can win there, he can win anywhere. With the United States lacking anything approaching a superstar since Nicklaus and Tom Watson, artists (hero-worshippers like most of the rest of us) have been attracted to these European golfers, and Severiano Ballesteros more than anyone.

Nevertheless, the United States remains easily the mightiest of individual golfing nations, and its golfers will do their best to ensure that the near-equality enjoyed at present by the Europeans and the Australians does not last long. On the other hand, one could point to the golf boom in every European country where golf is firmly established. Sweden, for example, has far more than its fair share of tennis superstars – and only occasional tournament winners at golf – surely it must soon produce top golfers. At the beginning of the 1990s, besides the British Isles, only Spain has made a really substantial contribution to Ryder Cup teams. From the rest of Europe only Bernhard Langer has made an impact.

American women players did not come to dominate the international game quite as quickly as their male counterparts. The great Glenna Collett in the 1920s could not extend her United States successes to Britain, where Cecil Leitch and, more so, Joyce Wethered, were the *non pareilles*. However, despite occasional British successes in the Curtis Cup, since about the mid-1930s, the best women players have been almost exclusively American. There is a European women's professional tour but if American women should choose to enter an event in force, they would very likely take nine of the top ten places. If this dominance fades, it will not be in this century.

It is in photographs far more than in paintings that the players of the recent past and of today have been recorded. Action golf photography started around 1890. Few pictures were taken, and as one would expect, even fewer have survived. Hardly any survive in negative form. But, even if very much hampered by slow film, the rudiments of golf photography were mastered very early on by such men as Moncrieff and Ullyiet. By early in the present century, the camera had progressed enormously and shutter speeds of well over 1/1000th of a second were available.

Fast film and lenses were not. Today they are the two basic tools of the golf photographer. Film quality improves almost yearly as regards speed and, more importantly, fineness of grain and colour correctness, improvements which the photographer these days takes almost for granted.

The most important tool of all is the fast telephoto lens. This dates from only the mid-1970s when the first 300 and 400mm lenses began to appear. On the other hand, and perhaps surprisingly, the variety of zoom lenses now available are little used. The quality of the resultant photograph is poorer, and the lower lens speed means that considerably brighter light is needed for truly effective results.

It remains true that a good single lens reflex camera, with both shutter speeds and exposures precisely measured, will serve the skilful photographer quite as well as the latest

Pebble Beach, California, Peter Cost

The landscape painter James Peter Cost (b.1923) comes from the Monterey Peninsula in California, and, not surprisingly, found his way to the marvellous Pebble Beach course. This is the 8th green, a hole which some would rate as the world's greatest par 4. Jack Nicklaus, for instance, considers the approach to the green 'the finest second shot on any golf course I have seen'. You can see why from this painting. The green is ringed by bunkers and there's a fall down to the Pacific along the front and to the right.

In addition, there is a long carry over the inlet of about 180 yards – that is, if you judge your tee shot correctly and finish close up to the edge of that precipice (marked by the yellow stake). If you are a little fearful of being long and decide on caution, you make the second shot even more frightening.

Pebble Beach was designed by a golfer with championship achievements at state level, Jack Neville. When complimented on his outstanding work, he modestly replied, 'The golf course was there all the time. All I did was find the holes.' What he meant was that the coastline was so spectacular that a visual delight was inevitable. The territory was superb, but Neville made the very best of it, producing one of golf's masterpieces, one many people consider the best in the world.

fully automatic products. Judgement of light, where you position yourself, and capturing the moment are what really count.

Photography even dominates painting. Painters who attempt portraiture, for example, depicting ultimate tensions on the 72nd green, seem all too often now to paint from still photographs or video recordings.

It remains different, however, in the area where golf painting really began – scenes where golfers are decorative incidental figures, there only to enhance the perspective of landscapes. Today, there are many competent workers in oil, watercolour and other mediums with the flair to convey the feel of the places where golf is played – and never much mind the insignificant figures who do it.

St Cloud, de Fanch Ledon
De Fanch Ledon may have been attracted to paint this charming view of the famous St Cloud course near Paris because of the growing popularity of the game.

It is only recently that golf has really taken off in France. Its earlier chic image may have limited its appeal, and it was also regarded as an Anglo-Saxon game, despite the evidence of 17th- and 18th-century prints of the game's precursor and near-relative.

Ben Hogan, 1953

Ben Hogan is on most people's shortlists for the title of the greatest golfer of all time, but it was not obvious from the outset that he would achieve such eminence. After turning professional in 1931, he had such little success on the fledgling U.S. Tour that he gave it up until 1937. He scarcely fared any better then. Then in 1940, contrary to previous form, he became the leading money-winner. He came back after the war with new determination and this earned him the U.S. PGA in 1946. In 1948 he won the event again, and added to it the first of his four U.S. Opens. Many people attributed his change of fortune to his conquering a snap hook that often devastated his younger game.

Instruction from Ben Hogan, Frank Williams, 1949

Early in 1949 Ben Hogan was badly hurt in a collision with a bus. It was thought, at first, that he was dead, but he eventually made a long-drawn-out and only partial recovery. Even so, he was able to return to his position as the world's greatest golfer during the early 1950s. These Frank Williams' cartoons for the Free Press *date from spring 1949, when Hogan must have felt well enough to resume his activities. He did not play any tournament golf until the following year. Since Hogan many other top golfers have been persuaded to give the benefit of their advice to readers of golfing magazines, with or without cartoon figures, but usually in illustrations.*

Ben Hogan Takes the British Open, 1953, Bill Brauer

Ben Hogan was not interested in playing golf in Britain, which during his career was small time compared to the game in the United States. In 1953, however, he won the Masters and the U.S. Open, and to take three majors in a year would be almost as great a feat as Jones' 1930 Grand Slam. Besides this, others were urging him that to win on a links course would set the final seal on his greatness. Hogan filed his entry for the British Open, held that year at Carnoustie on the windy east coast of Scotland, the most feared Open venue of them all. He gave himself plenty of time to prepare and won with the unusual descending scores of 73, 71, 70 and 68.

Hogan never entered another British Open, and played in Britain only once again when he represented the United States with Sam Snead in the Canada (now World) Cup at Wentworth. They won.

Stymied, 1940s
This advertisement for Schweppes soft drinks (sodas) depicts a stymie. The stymie was to be abolished in 1951, but before then, was the cause of many hard-luck stories in golf matchplay. If your opponent's ball finished between you and the hole, you had to loft over it or be content to putt past it but not directly at the hole, accepting that two putts would be needed. One of the great golf matches, between Bobby Jones and Cyril Tolley, in the 1930 Amateur Championship at St Andrews, was settled when Jones accidentally laid Tolley a stymie on the 19th.

'That's Amoré', from The Caddy, 1953
Neither the song nor the film were great hits, but they do serve to remind us of the association, popular with artists earlier in the century, between golf and affairs of the heart.

(Above) **Eisenhower, Malenkov and Caddie, B. Borsis, c.1954**
President Eisenhower was well known for his love of golf, so he provided cartoonists with a ready subject for their comments. Georgi Malenkov was the Prime Minister of the Soviet Union for only a short time, from 1953 to 1955, and objected strongly to the re-arming of what was then West Germany. President Eisenhower scores a hole in one because of the NATO involvement.

(Left) **'Oh! What a Lie!', anon, 1950s**
George Washington may never have told a lie but, reincarnated as a caddie, he knew that golfers do. This drawing was the original artwork for a postcard.

(Left) 'H.M. McDuff Regarding American Visitor', Frank Reynolds, 1950s
The cartoonist and illustrator Frank Reynolds drew golf subjects through much of his working life. With the post-war U.S. supremacy at the highest level, it might be assumed that quite ordinary club players were also much better than they actually were. 'Yon's some kind of a killer. Says he shot 80 at North Berwick.'

(Right) **Potters Bar Golf Club, Gerald Robert Tucke, 1970**
This impressionistic sketch in watercolours depicts a course to the north of London. Potters Bar may not be one of the great clubs, but the painting shows how the tradition of artists being attracted by the peacefulness of golf courses has survived into the modern era.

(Left) **'Would You Mind Keeping Your Eye on My Ball, Major MacDangle?' Emmwood, 1965**
Here we have the golfing military gentleman again (see Bateman's cartoon, page 173). He has been inveigled into playing golf with a shapely young woman. She wants him to follow the flight of her golf ball, but he is more interested in flighty thoughts of a different nature.

The 18th – St Andrews, Robert Wade
The 18th green at St Andrews is hallowed ground, and the clubhouse probably the single most famous building in the golfing world. Robert Wade depicts the scene as evening shadows lengthen and shower clouds retreat. He is amongst Australia's leading artists, a keen golfer himself, and one of the best-known of the painters now turning their attention, reviving a century-old tradition, to the landscapes of golf.

Golf Course, painting by Mike Vaughan, 1980s

This painting, which dates from the mid 1980s, took its inspiration from one of the many golf courses constructed in Spain and Portugal in recent years. Often in spectacular locations, and drawing on the skills of the finest golf architects, these courses have proved hugely popular for golfing holdiays. Their development has paralleled the rapid progress of Spanish golf in recent years, spearheaded by Severiano Ballesteros.

Play-off for the 1962 U.S. Open, Bill Brauer
The 1962 U.S. Open was at Oakmont and was settled by a play-off between Jack Nicklaus (centre) and Arnold Palmer (to his left). By this time, Palmer had become a hugely popular American hero, while Nicklaus, who had been an immensely promising amateur, had only recently turned professional. Nicklaus' win did not go down well with the public, and for a good many years Palmer stayed everybody's favourite to Nicklaus' detriment.

In this play-off Nicklaus first showed what a threat he was to Palmer's supremacy, winning 71 to 74.

In another U.S. Open five years later, the pair were level after three rounds and again Nicklaus came through with a 65 over Palmer's 69.

Cigarette Cards: Tom Watson, Gary Player, Lee Trevino, 1970s

Cigarette cards disappear from time to time and seem to be extinct, then a company starts issuing them again, much to the delight of collectors. They give caricaturists the opportunity to capture distinctive features or mannerisms in a snappy and immediate form.

TOM WATSON

LEE TREVINO

GARY PLAYER

(Right) The Masters: Nick Faldo and Jack Nicklaus, Paul Gribble, 1990

Nick Faldo on his way to winning the Masters in 1990. Faldo had won it in 1989 as well, and so became one of the two players in history, and the only Briton, to win the event in consecutive years. Nicklaus' caddie is tending a bag with the name of the golf club manufacturer MacGregor clearly visible on the side. This is a nice example of reverse sponsorship and of the large sums of money to be made out of the game today. After years of using MacGregor clubs and being paid by the company to sport its name, Nicklaus eventually bought the company himself.

Norman at Augusta, Edgar Barnett, 1987
The Australian Greg Norman won the 1986 British Open in convincing style at Turnberry. Although he is undoubtedly an international superstar, that remains the only major championship on his record. It could be that he will eventually go down in history more for the majors he threw away with one bad shot, or which were snatched away from him by someone else's outrageous luck rather than his own shortcomings.

In 1986, for instance, he could have won all four majors. At Augusta in the Masters, he hit his iron to the final green well right, thus losing the chance of a play-off with Jack Nicklaus.

In the U.S. Open, he led after the second and third round but then played relatively poorly. Then came his British Open success. Shortly after, he went on to dominate the PGA Championship, leading by four shots after each round. He began to stagger on the second nine of the final round with three bogeys and two double bogeys. Even so, he was level with Bob Tway as they played the final hole and Norman then hit easily the better drive and was on the edge of the green with his second shot, while Tway was in a greenside bunker. It seemed that Norman was going to do it after all the stumbles. With that, Tway, about 15 yards from the hole, sent his ball straight in from the sand. Another major gone! It was bad luck at the last gasp, but Norman should never have allowed Tway to get close.

With memories of that fluke shot no doubt still in his mind, Norman came to Augusta for the 1987 Masters. For the first 36 holes he played untidy golf, but a third round 66 brought him up to a shot off the pace. On the last day, he played steadily and came close to winning when a 5 yard putt on the final hole missed by a whisker.

He was into a sudden death play-off with Seve Ballesteros and Larry Mize. We see them here in this painting. Ballesteros, in a light blue shirt, is on the left; Mize, in a visor, is marking his ball. Norman has been a little unlucky. His second shot was at the flag but did not bite and ran through to the back of the green. Ballesteros then took three putts and departed for the clubhouse in tears. Mize and Norman moved on to the 11th. Mize played his second shot first. Wanting to keep well clear of the lake at the left of the green, he overdid it and went well right, perhaps 20 yards off the green and about 50 yards from the flag. Norman played a little right also, but was comfortably on the green. Mize had little chance of getting down in two more from where he was; Norman had every chance of getting down in two putts for the Masters. As he considered his first putt, Larry Mize ended it all. His pitch and run went into the hole. It was the most outrageous shot ever to win a major championship.

Arnold Palmer

The charisma of Arnold Palmer in his prime has only been equalled since by Severiano Ballesteros. Both had, or have, their armies of supporters whenever they appear in competition, but Palmer's influence on golf was the more decisive. His appeal did much to energize the U.S. Tour when it was flagging in popularity after Sam Snead and Ben Hogan had begun to wane in the 1950s. His first appearances in the British Open championship from 1960 did much to set the event on its way to becoming the world championship of golf. When he turned 50, the U.S. Senior Tour was also electrified and is now almost as successful as the main Tour. Under the skilful management of Mark McCormack, Palmer made, and continues to make, an enormous income from his golfing fame.

In the photograph of Palmer driving at the 1st in the 1985 PGA at Cherry Hills, Denver he is almost incidental, with the spectators lining the fairway and a vivid sky making a strong contribution. Both hole and course have great significance in Palmer's career. Starting out on his final round in the 1960 U.S. Open, Palmer was well behind but he felt that he still had a good chance of winning – if he could shoot a 65. One key to that was driving the 1st for a two-putt birdie. He had been trying to start his round that way throughout the Open, but had got into trouble. This time he brought it off and was on his way. He got the 65 and won. This victory was not the start, but it established him as a superstar.

David Cannon's portrait is a recent photograph of the great man, showing him as countless numbers see him on the U.S. Senior Tour.

Jack Nicklaus

Who is the greatest player in the history of the game? A golfer can beat only those people who play against him in his own times. For many of those who have seen generations of golfers, Jack Nicklaus would be their nomination. His total of 20 major championships leaves Bobby Jones, another strong contender for the title, far behind with 13. But Jones had had enough by 1930 when he was only 28, while Nicklaus continues to play into his fifties. Perhaps, as has been done with boxing, someone will feed a computer with statistics and playing analyses for it to decide between the claims of Young Tom Morris, Harry Vardon, Bobby Jones, Ben Hogan, Byron Nelson and Jack Nicklaus. Until that day (assuming we are convinced by its decision), we have to content ourselves with the thought that Nicklaus was, at his peak, the finest player around.

He is seen here on his way to his 1986 victory in the Masters, almost certainly his last major victory, which was also his first since 1980. For a bunker shot, the photographer should try to place himself in front and on line with the golfer's target. Here Nicklaus is framed in part by sand, and the ball has also been caught in the frame.

Lee Trevino

With the possible exception of Walter Hagen, Lee Trevino is the most unorthodox of the great players. He stands wide open to the target, has a hooker's grip, yet tries to play with consistent fade. A relatively short driver, he keeps the ball in play and is excellent on and around the greens.

He was an unknown when he won the 1968 U.S. Open and was thought to have poor technique. His record, however, shows that it worked for him, and he is among the top money winners of all time and making a new fortune in Senior golf.

Trevino has always thought it part of his duties to entertain, and maintains a constant stream of banter on course.

(Left) **Tom Watson**
For quite a while, Tom Watson was thought to lack star appeal. He retorted, 'Charisma is winning major championships.' He was right. Watson has won the British Open five times, two Masters and one U.S. Open. Not the superb putter he once was and into his forties, he will probably not add more than a win or two to his record – but he was the man who replaced Jack Nicklaus as the greatest current player in the game.

A delightfully brisk player, he would be a personal choice as one of a fourball to get around a golf course at a proper speed. The other three players might be Lanny Wadkins, Fuzzy Zoeller (the fastest), and Lee Trevino. Tommy Armour, the original slow golfer, once said, 'Whoever said that golf was supposed to be played fast?' Nevertheless, there is a lot of pleasure to be gained from watching Watson's business-like approach. He is seen here driving from the 15th tee at St Andrews in 1990.

(Right) **Raymond Floyd**
Rather a playboy in his youth, Floyd matured into a very solid figure, with a career occupying much the same time span as Jack Nicklaus (1963 to the present). Although without Nicklaus' overall record, he secured his place in the history books when he became the oldest player to win the U.S. Open in 1981. The record was short-lived; it was beaten by Hale Irwin in 1990. Floyd has also won two PGA championships and a Masters. He was widely praised for his captaincy of the 1989 U.S. Ryder Cup team, which tied with a strong European team flushed by their success two years previously.

Floyd usually prefers to use a longer-than-standard putter. He dislikes crouching over the ball like Ballesteros and like golfers at the turn of the century. A longer putter also enables him to strike the ball more gently.

(Left) Curtis Strange
The late 1980s found the United States searching for a new golf superstar. For a time it seemed that Curtis Strange could be the man, especially after he won consecutive U.S. Opens in 1988 and 1989. He was also the leading money winner in 1985, 1987 and 1988, a position far more highly prized in the United States than in Europe. After that, he was rather less successful but, as he will not reach the age of 40 until 1995, he has time left to make a renewed impact.

Curtis Strange was once better known for winning money than titles but eventually this changed, earning him the nickname 'Iron Man' from his fellow pros. The reasons for this became apparent when he won his two U.S. Opens and also at the climax of the 1989 Ryder Cup at The Belfry, when he overhauled Ian Woosnam on the last three holes, his victory enabling the United States to tie the match.

Golf is a game of both agony and ecstasy. Here, at the 1990 British Open, Strange is very pleased indeed to have holed out from a bunker.

(Right) Payne Stewart
The current most likely U.S. candidate for greatness, Payne Stewart, has, by late 1991, two major titles on his record and is after more. At the 1991 Open Championship, Britain's Steven Richardson made a deliberate point, when paired with Stewart, of going out on the course looking as drab as possible – grey trousers and dull blue short-sleeved shirt. But the photographers warmed to whatever U.S. football team colours Stewart was wearing.

Stewart is far less dramatic in his play than in his attire. He has a very sound swing, is highly competent with all the shots from tee to green, and an excellent putter.

The clothing here is typical, with the photograph capturing the moment of triumph as he holes a putt.

Greg Norman

The Australian Greg Norman is undoubtedly one of golf's superstars and a huge earner – from his looks as well as from his golf. He achieved this without piling up the major titles that one might have expected. He has twice been the leading money earner on the U.S. Tour, without winning either the Open or the Masters, and has enjoyed great success worldwide, although the 1986 British Open at Turnberry remains his only major.

Nicknamed 'The Great White Shark' because of his sun-bleached hair and reputed passion for big game fishing, Norman is at ease with this image and enhances it by ownership of very fast cars. Backlighting of the hair is part of the success of this picture.

Nick Faldo
In 1990, Nick Faldo was the world's leading golfer, winning both the Masters and the British Open. This Open victory was perhaps his finest performance. After two rounds, he and Australian Greg Norman were well out in front, with equal record totals of 132. Faldo then dominated the rest of the championship, having 'destroyed' Norman in the third round when they played together.

He now has a claim to be considered the finest-ever British golfer, and is certainly the best since the days of the Great Triumvirate, just ahead of Henry Cotton.

He is shown here en route to his 1990 Masters title. The spectators have been deliberately thrown out of focus so that the golfer dominates the scene.

Severiano Ballesteros

With over 60 victories on his record worldwide, the Spaniard is the most international of modern stars. For spectator appeal, in Europe at least, he is unmatched. Even at a run-of-the-mill tournament, if Seve is in contention, the gate is likely to be doubled.

Like Palmer, he brings great intensity to his play and lets the emotions flow freely. But part of Palmer's appeal was that his swing was not pretty. Although the ball usually did the right things, spectators could still feel – despite Palmer's awesome power – that they could swing the golf club as well as he did. Ballesteros has a very elegant swing indeed. He reaches a beautiful position at the finish and always seems ideally balanced throughout. (There are occasional exceptions, such as when he is trying to carve his ball out of a bush or produce an extravagant hook or slice!)

Here, he is at sun-baked Troon during the 1989 British Open, punching in a short iron at the 8th or Postage Stamp hole. Taken a split second later, the photographer would have lost the face as Ballesteros moved into his follow-through with the head coming up. The dust of impact is flying, and we can see the ball on its way to the target.

INDEX

PICTURE CREDITS

The publishers are grateful to the following, who kindly supplied photographs for inclusion in this book:
Allsport: 196, 196–7, 198, 199, 200 (right), 201, 202 (left), 203, 204, 204–5
Sarah Baddiel: 37, 39 (bottom), 40, 42 (right), 58, 62, 67, 68, 69, 73, 80, 85, 86, 87, 91, 92, 93, 95, 96, 97, 98, 99, 101, 102, 103, 108, 109, 111, 112, 113, 114, 117, 118, 119, 122, 123, 124, 125, 129, 130, 131, 132, 133, 134, 135, 136, 137, 138, 139, 140, 141, 142, 143, 144, 145, 146, 147, 148, 149, 150, 152, 153, 154, 156, 157, 158, 159, 160, 161, 162, 163, 164, 165, 166, 167, 168, 170, 171, 172, 175 (left), 179, 181, 182, 183, 184 (left), 187, 191, 192
Burlington Gallery Ltd: 41, 126, 127, 188–9
Christie's: 32, 83, 110
Galerie 1900–2000: 142, 180, 184 (right)
The Golf Shop Collection (P.O. Box 14609, Cincinnati, Ohio 45250, USA): 7, 29, 34–5, 60, 63, 69, 70, 90, 105, 116, 128, 155, 174, 177, 178, 194–5
Paul Gribble/The Wingfield Sporting Gallery London 193
The Michael Hobbs Golf Collection: 3, 16, 17, 18, 22, 25, 26, 27, 36, 49, 200 (left), 202 (right)
Hulton-Deutsch 84
National Portrait Gallery of Scotland, Edinburgh: 21
Phillips (London and Chester): 31, 38, 44, 48, 59, 64, 151, 186
Phillips (New York): 57
Phillips (Scotland): 30, 39 (top left and right), 72, 82–3, 173
The Frank Reynolds Golf Collection: 170, 171, 185
Felix Rosenstiel's Widow and Son Ltd: 190
Sotheby's: 20, 42 (left), 61, 81, 151, 175

We are also grateful to Luffness and Gullane Golf Clubs for supplying subjects to be photographed, to the kind generosity of a private collector, and to Bill Burnett for taking the photographs.